A System-Theoretic Safety Engineering Approach for Software-Intensive Systems

A System-Theoretic Safety Engineering Approach for Software-Intensive Systems

Von der Fakultät Informatik, Elektrotechnik und Informationstechnik der Universität Stuttgart zur Erlangung der Würde eines Doktors der Naturwissenschaften (Dr. rer. nat.) genehmigte Abhandlung

Vorgelegt von

Asim Abdulkhaleq

geboren in Taiz, Jemen

Hauptberichter: Prof. Dr. Stefan Wagner

Mitberichter: Prof. Dr. Nancy Leveson (MIT)

Tag der mündlichen Prüfung: 06.02.2017

Institut für Softwaretechnologie

2017

Bibliografische Information der Deutschen Nationalbibliothek
Die Deutsche Nationalbibliothek verzeichnet diese Publikation in der Deutschen Nationalbibliografie; detaillierte bibliografische Daten sind im Internet über http://dnb.d-nb.de abrufbar.
1. Aufl. - Göttingen: Cuvillier, 2017
Zugl.: Stuttgart, Univ., Diss., 2017

D93 (Diss. Universität Stuttgart)

Nonnenstieg 8, 37075 Göttingen
Telefon: 0551-54724-0
Telefax: 0551-54724-21
www.cuvillier.de

1. Auflage, 2017
Gedruckt auf umweltfreundlichem, säurefreiem Papier aus nachhaltiger Forstwirtschaft.

ISBN 978-3-7369-9492-8
eISBN 978-3-7369-8492-9

Dedication

This PhD research Thesis is dedicated to my best friend Redwan Alakori who passed away on Saturday, 08.10.2016 because of an elevator accident in Cairo, Egypt.

Abstract

Software safety is a crucial aspect during the development of modern safety-critical systems. However, safety is a system level property, and therefore, *software safety* must be considered at the system-level to ensure the whole system's safety [Lev11]. In fact, making software safe is more than just identifying software hazards. The software components in the systems need also to be verified extensively against their safety requirements to ensure a high level of system safety. The complexity of software systems makes it difficult to define appropriate software safety requirements with traditional safety analysis techniques such as FTA (Fault Tree Analysis) [Ves+81], FMEA (Failure Mode and Effects Analysis) [Mil49]. To cope with complex systems, a new technique called STPA (System-Theoretic Process Analysis)[Lev11] based on system and control theory has been developed by Leveson.

In the software development process, formal verification and functional testing are complementary approaches which are used to verify the functional correctness of software; however, even perfectly reliable software could lead to an accident [Won+10; Lev11]. The correctness of software cannot ensure the safe operation of safety-critical software systems. Therefore, developing safety-critical software requires a more systematic software and safety engineering process that enables the software and safety engineers to recognize the potential software risks. For this purpose, this dissertation introduces a comprehensive safety engineering approach based on STPA for Software-Intensive Systems, called *STPA SwISs* [AWL15], which provides seamless STPA safety analysis and software safety verification activities to allow the software and safety engineers to work together during the software development for safety-critical systems and help them to recognize the associated software risks at the system level.

To explore and evaluate the application of the STPA SwISs approach, we conducted a pilot case study and two industrial case studies based on automotive software systems. The pilot case study was conducted during the development of a software simulator of the Adaptive Cruise Control System (ACC) with a stop-and-go function using a Lego-Mindstorms EV3 robot. The first industrial case study was conducted on the Active Cruise Control System (ACC) at BMW Group. The second case study was conducted on the fully Automated Driving system (AD) of autonomous vehicles at Continental. The results demonstrate the effectiveness of the STPA SwISs approach and show that it is scalable and applicable to real-world software systems.

We also developed a safety engineering platform called XSTAMPP to support the application of STAMP methodologies and the STPA SwISs approach to help software and safety engineers to identify the software safety requirements, automatically verify their design and implementation against the STPA-generated software safety requirements with model checking tools and automatically generate safety-based test cases from STPA results.

As a conclusion, we believe that the combination of the STPA-based safety analysis and the safety-based software verification activities is a practical and effective way to recognize software risks and assure the quality of software. The degree of automation added value to the proposed approach by allowing the safety and software engineers to perform seamless safety analysis, software safety verification and safety-based testing activities in one comprehensive approach. Furthermore, this dissertation opens doors for interesting opportunities in software safety engineering.

ZUSAMMENFASSUNG

Software-Sicherheit ist ein entscheidender Aspekt bei der Entwicklung moderner sicherheitskritischer Systeme. Er betrifft die Sicherheit des gesamten Systems und muss daher auch auf Systemebene behandelt werden. Das Erkennen von Software-Risiken allein reicht indes nicht aus, um die Sicherheit einer Software zu gewährleisten. Vielmehr müssen die Software-Komponenten des Systems auch umfassend gegen die Sicherheitsanforderungen des Gesamtsystems geprüft werden, um ein hohes Maß an Systemsicherheit zu erreichen. Aufgrund der Komplexität von Software-Systemen ist es schwierig, mit traditionellen Analyseverfahren wie FTA (Fault Tree Analysis) oder FMEA (Failure Mode and Effects and Analysis) geeignete Software-Sicherheitsanforderungen zu definieren. Ein neues Verfahren zur Analyse komplexer Systeme ist die 2004 von Nancy Leveson entwickelte, auf einem systemtheoretischen Unfallmodell basierende Systemtheoretische Prozessanalyse (STPA).

Bei der Software-Entwicklung sind formale Verifikation und Tests einander ergänzende Ansätze, um die funktionale Korrektheit von Software zu prüfen. Doch könnte es bei selbst vollkommen zuverlässiger Software zu Unfällen kommen. Selbst bei absolut korrekter Software ist kein sicherer Betrieb sicherheitskritischer Software-Systeme gewährleistet. Daher erfordert die Entwicklung sicherheitskritischer Software einen systematischeren Prozess bei der sicherheitstechnischen und der Software-Entwicklung, der die Entwickler befähigt, potenzielle Software-Risiken zu erkennen. Die vorliegende Dissertation stellt ein umfassendes, auf STPA für Software-intensive Systeme basierendes Software-Sicherheitsverfahren namens STPA SwISs vor. Dieses Verfahren stellt verschiedene Maßnahmen für STPA-Sicherheitsanalysen und die Software-Sicherheitsverifikation bereit, die es Software- und Sicherheitstechnikern ermöglichen, bei der Software-Entwicklung für sicherheitskritische Systeme zusammenzuarbeiten und die damit verbundenen Software-Risiken auf Systemebene zu erkennen.

Um den Einsatz des STPA-SwISs-Verfahrens zu erforschen und zu bewerten, wurden ein Pilotprojekt sowie zwei Fallstudien in der Industrie durchgeführt, beide an Software-Systemen für die Automobilindustrie. Die Pilotstudie wurde während der Entwicklung des Prototyps eines Software-Simulators des

Abstandsregeltempomaten (ACC) mit Stop-and-Go-Funktion mit einem Lego-Mindstorms-EV3-Roboter durchgeführt, die erste Fallstudie in der Industrie am Abstandsregeltempomaten (ACC) bei der BMW Group. Die zweite Fallstudie untersuchte das vollautomatische Fahrsystem (AD) selbstfahrender Fahrzeuge bei Continental. Die Ergebnisse sprechen für die Leistungsfähigkeit von STPA SwISs und zeigen, dass das Verfahren skalierbar und auf Systeme in der Praxis anwendbar ist.

Ferner wurde eine Plattform namens XSTAMPP verwendet, die die Anwendung von STAMP-Methoden und von STPA SwISs unterstützt und Software- und Sicherheitstechnikern bei der Identifizierung von Sicherheitsanforderungen hilft, indem sie deren Entwürfe und Implementierungen anhand der von STPA generierten Sicherheitsanforderungen unter Einsatz von Model-Checking-Werkzeugen überprüft und auf Basis der STPA-Ergebnisse automatisch Testfälle generiert.

Unsere Schlussfolgerung lautet, dass die Kombination der Analyse auf STPA-Basis mit den sicherheitstechnischen Software-Verifikationsverfahren eine zweckmäßige und effektive Möglichkeit bietet, Software-Risiken zu erkennen und Software-Qualität zu gewährleisten. Der Automatisierungsgrad verbesserte den vorgeschlagenen Ansatz, denn dadurch war es Software-und Sicherheitstechnikern möglich, die Sicherheitsanalyse, die Software-Sicherheitsverifikation sowie Softwaretests mit demselben umfassenden Verfahren durchzuführen. Darüber hinaus eröffnet diese Arbeit interessante Möglichkeiten in der Software-Sicherheitstechnik.

Acknowledgments

First of all, I would like to express my sincerest gratitude to my main advisor Prof. Dr. Stefan Wagner for giving me this opportunity to work with his group and under his guidance, motivation, collaboration, precious support, suggestions and ideas for making this dissertation possible. I appreciate his continuous motivation and support.

I would also like to express my deepest gratitude to my co-advisor Prof. Dr. Nancy Leveson for developing the STAMP model, making a safer world, believing in me, giving me the opportunity to work under her supervision, and accepting my works to be presented at the annual STAMP MIT meetings. Without her feedback, comments and suggestions throughout my work, this dissertation would not have been possible.

My warm thanks go to the researcher at MIT, Dr. John Thomas for his feedback, suggestions and support.

I am grateful to the current researchers and employees in the software engineering group that I collaborate with them in daily work, teaching courses and academic publications. Ivan Bogicevic, Jan-Peter Ostberg, Jasmin Ramadani, Daniel Kulesz, Kai Mindermann, Erica Weilemann, Wolfgang Fechner, Kornelia Kuhle, Horst Vöhringer, Verena Käfer, Yang Wang, Rainer Niedermayr and Daniel Graziotin. Sebastian Vöst was especially helpful in providing me the opportunity to evaluate my dissertation at BMW Group, Munich.

Special thanks to the researchers and employees at Continental, Regensburg and Frankfurt am Main, Daniel Lammering, Jürgen Röder, Norbert Balbierer, Ludwig Ramsauer, Thomas Raste, Hagen Boehmert, and Pierre Blueher for providing me the opportunity to work with them on assessing the architectural design of fully automated vehicles.

Thanks also to the graduate students who worked with me. Lukas Balzer, Aliaksei Babkovich, Adam Grahovac, Jarkko Heidenwag, Benedikt Markt, Jaqueline Patzek, Sebastian Sieber, Fabian Toth, Patrick Wickenhaeuser, Yannic Sowoidnich, Martin Root, Dennis Maseluk, Ting Luk-He and Domas Mikalkinas.

I am grateful for the help from Dr. Rick Kuhn, National Institute of Standards and Technology, USA, who provides me the Automated Combinatorial Testing tool (ACTS).

Last, but certainly not least, my sincerest gratitude goes to my own family, especially my deceased parents. Their memories will be with me always and I will be ever grateful for their assistance. My wife Nada Alsalami and my daughter Lamar Abdulkhaleq, who are giving me the happiness in every second in my life. My brother Dr. med. uni. Abdulrahman Al-Schameri and his family members, Anita Macheiner, Sami Al-Schameri, and Sarah Al-Schameri for supporting me throughout all my studies and living in Germany. They have been generous with their encouragement during my studies; I am indebted to them forever.

This dissertation would not have been possible without the support from my family, advisors, colleagues, industrial researchers and friends.

Stuttgart, February 2017
Asim Abdulkhaleq

Contents

List of Figures

List of Tables

List of Definitions

List of Abbreviations

A-CAST Automated CAST Tool Support

A-STPA Automated STPA Tool Support

ACC (Active) Adaptive Cruise Control Systems

ACTS Automated Combinatorial Testing for Software

AD Fully Automated Driving function

ANSI-C C Programming Language published by the American National Standards Institute and the International Organization for Standardization

BDD Binary Decision Diagram

CAST Causal Analysis based on STAMP

CTL Computation Tree Logic

FMEA Failure Mode and Effects Analysis

FMECA Failure Mode and Effect Criticality Analysis

GPS Global Positioning System

HAZOP Hazard and Operability Analysis

LTL Linear Temporal Logic

MBT Model-based Testing

NuSMV New Symbolic Model Verifier

Promela Process Meta Language

SBM Safe Behavioral Model

SFMEA Software Failure Mode and Effects Analysis

SFTA Software Fault Tree Analysis

SMV Symbolic Model Verifier

SpecTRM-RL Specification Tools and Requirements Methodology

SPIN Simple Promela Interpreter

STAMP System-Theoretic Accident Model and Processes

STM Safe Test Model

STPA SwISs STPA-based Approach for Software-Intensive Systems Including Formal Verification and Testing

STPA TCGenerator STPA Safety-Based Test Cases Generator

STPA Verifier Verifying STPA safety Requirements Tool Support

UI User Interface

XSTPA Extended Approach to STPA Tool Support

GLOSSARY

ACCIDENT Accident (Loss) results from inadequate enforcement of the behavioral safety constraints on the process [Lev11]. 29

ADAPTIVE CRUISE CONTROL SYSTEMS [SAE03] is an advanced version of the cruise control which allows a vehicleś cruise control autonomously adapt the vehicleś speed to the traffic environment. 126

ADAPTIVE CRUISE CONTROL SYSTEM WITH STOP-AND-GO [VN00] is an extended version of the normal adaptive cruise control system. It maintains a certain speed and keeps a safe distance from the vehicle ahead based on the radar sensors. 177

CONTEXT TABLE is the critical set of combinations of the process model variable values for each control action in the control structure diagram [Tho13] 38

HAZARD is a system state or set of conditions that, together with a particular set of worst-case environmental conditions, will lead to an accident [Lev11] 38

ISO 26262 (ROAD VEHICLES FUNCTIONAL SAFETY) is an international functional safety standard, which provides guidance, recommendation and argumentation for a safety driven product development in the automotive area[ISOv]. 179

SAFE TEST MODEL The safe test model is an extended finite state machine model which is automatically constructed from the safe behavioral model. 88

SAFETY-BASED TESTING is basically a type of testing in which the test activities such as test case generation and test execution are based on the information derived during the safety analysis process. It is also known in literature as “risk-based testing" 179

SOFTWARE SAFETY is defined as the discipline of software assurance that is a systematic approach to identifying, analyzing, tracking, mitigating, and controlling software hazards and hazardous functions (data and commands) to ensure safe operation within a system [NAS04]. 5

CHAPTER 1

INTRODUCTION

> *The primary safety problem in software-intensive systems is not software "failure" but the lack of appropriate constraints on software behavior.*
>
> — N. LEVESON

Given the rapid innovations in software and technology, many complex systems are becoming software intensive. Software-intensive systems are systems in which software interacts with other software, systems, devices, sensors and with people [Wir+08]. Software has become an indispensable part of many modern systems and often performs the main safety-critical functions. Software safety as stated in [Alb+99] is practically concerned with the software causal factors that are linked to individual hazards and ensured that the mitigation of each causal factor is traced from software requirements to design, implementation, and test. An unexpected behavior of software may lead to catastrophic results such as injury or loss of human life, damaged property or environmental disturbances. Therefore, it becomes essential to test the software components for unexpected behavior before using them in practice [Min91]. The Toyota Prius, the General Motors airbag and the loss of the Mars Polar Lander (MPL) mission [JPL00] are well-known software problems in which the software played an important role in the loss, although the software had been successfully verified against all functional requirements. Recently, Google's self-driving car and Tesla autopilot are the two latest software-related accidents in the automotive domain.

Many different safety analysis approaches exist. The most widely practiced safety analysis approaches are Fault Tree Analysis (FTA) [Ves+81], Failure Mode and Effect Criticality Analysis (FMECA) [FME67] and Hazard and Operability Analysis (HAZOP) [Tro68] which are developed over 50 years ago, before computers were common in engineered systems. As a result, these safety analysis methods do not completely ensure safety in complex systems. In such systems, the accidents are resulting when component failures, external disturbances, and/or dysfunctional interactions among system components are not adequately handled [Lev11]. A new trend is to advance safety analysis techniques using the system and control theory rather than the reliability theory. STAMP (System-Theoretic Accident Model and Processes) [Lev11] is a modern approach for safety engineering that promises to overcome the problems of the traditional safety analysis techniques. STPA (System-Theoretic Process Analysis) is designed for safety analysis in the system development and operating stages; the goal is to identify hazards existing in the system and provide safety constraints to mitigate those hazards.

1.1. Problem Statement

Safety is a system level property and, hence, needs to be analysed on the system level. Therefore, the software must fully satisfy the corresponding safety requirements which constrain the software from these behaviors that violate the safety of the whole system. Ensuring the safe operations of software involves that software must deal with hazardous behaviors which are identified by safety analysis at an early stage. STPA has been developed to derive detailed safety requirements for complex systems. However, STPA has not yet been placed into the software development process of safety-critical systems, and the current software engineering methods do not explicitly incorporate STPA safety activities. STPA safety analysis is often handled separately by the safety engineers, while software developers are usually not familiar with system safety analysis processes. Therefore, there is a gap between the software and safety engineering processes.

Moreover, the complexity of safety-critical software makes exhaustive software testing impossible. Therefore, we need to make sure that safety is sufficiently considered. Yet, many existing testing approaches and tools do not incorporate information from safety analysis. In case they do, they rely on traditional safety analysis techniques such as FTA and FMECA which focus on component failures instead of component interaction failures. A software safety testing approach integrated with alternative systems-theoretic safety analysis approaches such as STPA has been missing.

1.2. Research Objectives

This dissertation aims to fill the aforementioned gap to place STPA in the software engineering process to help software and safety engineers in deriving the appropriate software safety requirements, formally verifying them, generating safety-based test cases to recognize the associated software risks, and reduce them to a low level. Therefore, this dissertation has three main objectives. The first objective is to develop a comprehensive safety engineering approach which integrates the STPA safety analysis activities with the software verification activities in a software engineering development process such as the V-Model [FM91] to offer seamless safety analysis and verification. The second objective is to develop algorithms to automate the safety-based formal verification and testing activities of the proposed approach. Finally, this dissertation aims also at developing an open source tool to support the application of STAMP methodologies as well as the software verification activities based on the information derived during an STPA safety analysis.

1.3. Contributions

The thesis provides four contributions:

- **Developing a comprehensive safety engineering approach based on STPA to derive software safety requirements at the system level** [AWL15; AW14b; AW15a], formally verify them at the design and implementation levels, and generate safety-based test cases from the STPA results. The proposed approach has the following contributions: (1) We develop an algorithm based on STPA to derive unsafe software scenarios and automatically translate them into software safety constraints and specified them into a formal specification in LTL (Linear Temporal Logic) [Pnu77]. (2) We explore how to build a Safe Behavioral Model (SBM) based on the STPA control structure diagram and the process model. (3) We develop an algorithm to automatically extract the Safe Test Model (STM) from SBM model and check its correctness by automatically transforming it into a formal model such as an SMV (Symbolic Model Verifier) [McM93] and verify it against the STPA-generated safety requirements using the NuSMV model checker [Cim+00].

- **Providing formal definitions and algorithms for automation support** to the proposed approach (STPA SwISs), especially the document of STPA safety analysis results, automatically generate unsafe software scenarios based on the process model variables as well as automatically verify STPA software safety requirements and generate safety-based test cases.
- **Developing an open-source tool called XSTAMPP** to support the application of the STAMP methodologies as well as the STPA SwISs approach and enable the software and safety engineers to derive software safety requirements, automatically verify their software implementation and design against the STPA results and automatically generate safety-based test cases directly from the STPA results.
- **Evaluating the application of the STPA SwISs approach.** We conducted three case studies. The first case study is a pilot case study, which was conducted at our institute during developing a safe software simulator of the Adaptive Cruise Control (ACC) system with stop-and-go function to explore the application of the STPA SwISs approach during the development process of a safety-critical software. The second case study was conducted as an industrial case study at the German company BMW Group. We applied the proposed approach to BMW active cruise control system with stop-and-go function of the new car model G11. The case study was performed in the headquarter of BMW Group in Munich, Germany. The third case study was conducted as an industrial case study at the German company Continental. We first applied the STPA approach to the current project of the fully automated vehicle to evaluate and assess the architecture design of the fully automated vehicle. Then, we explored the application of the STPA SwISs approach at the software level of the fully automated vehicle to derive software safety requirements, automatically generate the unsafe software scenarios, translate them into software safety requirements and formalize the software safety requirements into formal specification in LTL to evaluate the architecture of the fully automated vehicles.

1.4. List of Publications

The following is a list of the publications which have been done to finish this work:

- Abdulkhaleq, A., Wagner, S. (2016) A Systematic and Semi-Automatic Safety-based Test Case Generation Approach Based on System-Theoretic Process Analysis. submitted to ACM Transactions on Software Engineering and Methodology.
- Abdulkhaleq, A., Sebastian, V., Wagner, S., Thomas, J. (2016) An Industrial Case Study on the Evaluation of a Safety Engineering Approach for Software-Intensive Systems in The Automotive Domain. Preprint. University of Stuttgart.
- Abdulkhaleq, A., Wagner, S., Lammering, D., Röder, J., Balbierer, N., Ramsauer, L., Raste, T., Boehmert, H. (2016) A Systematic Approach Based on STPA for Developing a Dependable Architecture for Fully Automated Driving Vehicles, in Proceeding of the Procedia Engineering Journal.
- Abdulkhaleq, A., Wagner, S. (2016) XSTAMPP 2.0: New Improvements to XSTAMPP Including CAST *Accident* Analysis and an Extended Approach to STPA. 2016 STAMP Conference at Massachusetts Institute of Technology (MIT), 21 March 2016, Boston, USA.
- Abdulkhaleq, A., Wagner, S., Leveson, N. (2015) A Comprehensive Safety Engineering Approach for Software-Intensive Systems Based on STPA, Procedia Engineering, Volume 128, 2015, Pages 2-11, ISSN 1877-7058.
- Abdulkhaleq, A., Wagner, S. (2015) Integrated Safety Analysis Using System-Theoretic Process Analysis and Software Model Checking. In Computer Safety, Reliability, and Security (Safecomp2015), Lecture Notes in Computer Science, Springer International Publishing, Delft, Netherlands (22-25 September 2015)
- Abdulkhaleq, A., Wagner, S. (2015) XSTAMPP: An eXtensible STAMP Platform As Tool Support for Safety Engineering. 2015 STAMP Conference at Massachusetts Institute of Technology (MIT), 26 March 2015, Boston, USA.

- Abdulkhaleq, A., Wagner, S. (2014) A Software Safety Verification Method Based on System-Theoretic Process Analysis. In Computer Safety, Reliability, and Security (Safecomp2014), Lecture Notes in Computer Science, Springer International Publishing, Vol. 8696, pp. 401-412.
- Abdulkhaleq, A., Wagner, S. (2014) A-STPA: An Open Tool Support for System-Theoretic Process Analysis. 2014 STAMP Conference at Massachusetts Institute of Technology (MIT), 27 March 2014, Boston, USA.
- Abdulkhaleq, A., Wagner, S. (2013) Experiences with Applying STPA to Software-Intensive Systems in the Automotive Domain". 2013 STAMP Conference at MIT, Boston, USA.
- Abdulkhaleq, A., Wagner, S. (2013) Integrating State Machine Analysis with System-Theoretic Process Analysis (STPA). Multikonferenz Software Engineering 2013 (SE 2013), ZeMoSS - Zertifizierung und modellgetriebene Entwicklung sicherer Software, Aachen, Germany pp. 501-514

1.5. Outline

The remainder of this dissertation is organised as follows: In Chapter 2, we present the background of this dissertation, including software safety challenges, traditional and modern safety analysis techniques and software verification and testing approaches. The state of the art is presented in Chapter 3. In Chapter 4, we presented our proposed approach for software safety engineering based on STPA including software testing and verification activities. Chapter 5 presents the automation support to the proposed approach. The tool support of the proposed approach is presented in Chapter 6. Chapter 7 presents the empirical validation, which introduces three cases studies on evaluating the application of the proposed approach: pilot case study and the two industrial case studies. In Chapter 8, we conclude the dissertation and present the future work.

CHAPTER 2

BACKGROUND

> *It's hard enough to find an error in your code when you're looking for it; it's even harder when you've assumed your code is error-free.*
>
> — *STEVE MCCONNELL*

2.1. Software Safety Challenges

Software is an integral and increasingly complex part of modern safety critical systems (as shown in Figure 2.1). Therefore, it is essential to analyse software safety in a system context to gain a comprehensive understanding of the roles of software and to identify the software-related risks that can cause hazards in the system. Leveson [Lev91] noted that software by itself is not hazardous and cannot directly cause damage to human life or the environment; it can only contribute to hazards in a system context. Software can create hazardous system states through erroneous control of the system or by misleading the system operators when taking actions [Lev11]. Software has no random failures and it does not wear out like hardware components [Lev91; Jaf+91]. Flaws in software are systematic failures which stem from flawed requirements, design errors or implementation flaws [Lev91; Jaf+91]. System hazards related to software are caused by software flaws, software specification errors and uncontrolled interactions among different components forming the system, rather than failures of single components [Har10].

Ensuring the safe operation of systems requires that the potential risks associated with increased reliance on software be well understood, so that they can be adequately controlled. To develop safe software, therefore, we first need

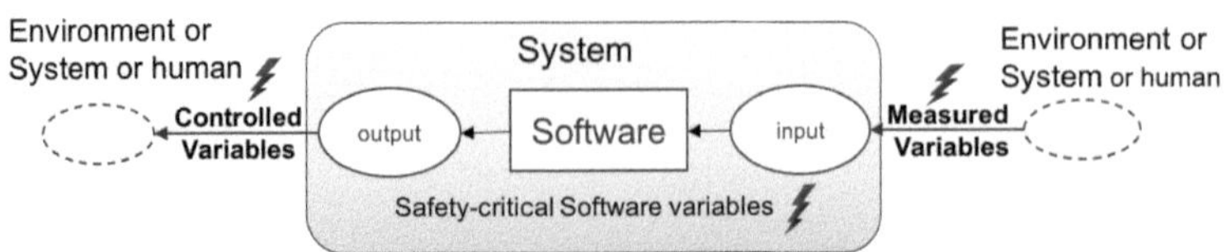

Figure 2.1.: Software is an integral part of system

to identify and analyse software-related hazards and the unsafe scenarios and develop the corresponding software safety requirements at the system level. To assure that these software-related unsafe scenarios cannot occur in a system, safety verification activities are required which include a demonstration of whether the software design and implementation meet those software safety requirements [NAS10]. However, the software safety requirements are written in natural languages. Therefore, to enable the software verification activities (e.g. testing and formal analysis), these requirements should be specified into a formal specification in Linear Temporal Logic (LTL).

2.2. Safety Analysis Techniques

Over the past seventy years, the most basic models of accident causation are the sequential models. The Domino model (sequential accident model) by Heinrich [Hei31] is one of the earliest accident causation models, proposed in 1931. The Domino model describes an accident as a chain of discrete events which occur in a particular temporal order [Fer88]. There are five safety factors which are addressed by the Domino model: 1) social environment, 2) fault of the human, 3) unsafe acts or conditions, 4) accident and 5) injury [Qur08]. Epidemiological accident models [Isk62] are meant to explain the accident causation in complex systems. These models are valuable because they provide a basis for discussing the complexity of accidents that overcomes the limitations of sequential models [Hol04]. The epidemiological models consider the events leading to accidents as analogous to the spreading of a disease. The epidemiological accident model can also be used to study causal relationships between environmental factors and accidents or diseases. An accident is conceived as the outcome of a combination of factors in this model. Some of the factors manifest and some are latent, but they happen to exist together in time and space [Rau13]. A famous example of epidemiological models is the Swiss Cheese model: It was proposed by Reason in the 1990's [Rea90] and emphasises the concept of organisational safety and how protection barriers may fail. The Swiss cheese model [Rea97; RHP06] views accidents much like the spreading of disease and describes the combination of latent conditions present in the system for some time and their role in unsafe acts made by operators.

2.2.1. Traditional Safety Analysis Techniques

There are over 100 different hazard analysis approaches in existence [Eri05]. Many of these approaches, however, are not widely practiced. Fault Tree Analysis (FTA), Failure Mode and Effect Analysis (FMEA) and Hazard and Operability Analysis (HAZOP) are most commonly used by system safety analysts. These approaches are known as traditional hazard analysis techniques in the academic literature, which rely on accident causation models which are sequential or epidemiological.

2.2.1.1. FTA

The Fault Tree Analysis Approach (FTA) [Ves+81] was developed at Bell Laboratories in the early 1960's under a U.S. Air Force contract to analyse the Minuteman missile system. FTA is a top-down approach to identify critical failure combinations. FTA is based on the chain of event accidents model. It is widely used to discover design defects during the development of a system and to investigate the causes of accidents or problems that occur during system operations [LN05; Lev82; LH83b]. The input of FTA is a known hazard, failure or accident, and a design description of the system under analysis. The FTA process can be divided into four main steps: 1) identify the root node (hazard or accident or failure); 2) identify the combination of events or conditions that caused the root node and combine them by using Boolean logic operators; 3) decompose the sub-nodes until events determined are basic (leaf nodes); and 4) identify minimum cut sets which are the smallest sets of basic events that cause the root node to occur.

2.2.1.2. FMEA and FMECA

The Failure Mode, Effects and Analysis Approach (FMEA) [Mil49] was first introduced by the U.S. military for weapons systems in 1949 as a systematic, procedure for evaluating and discovering the potential failures, their potential cause mechanisms and the risks designed into a product or a process. By the early 1970s FMEA was used in civil aviation and the automotive industry [FME67]. FMEA helps to identify where and how the component might fail and to assess the relative impact of different failures. FMEA is, similar to FTA, based on the chain of events accidents model. FMEA is a bottom-up, structured, table-based process for discovering and documenting the ways in which a component can fail and the consequences of those failures. The input to FMEA is a design description of the system and component. The FMEA process can be divided into four sub-tasks: 1) establish the scope of the analysis, 2) identify the failure modes of each block; 3) determine the effect of each potential failure mode and its potential causes; and 4) evaluate each failure mode in terms of the worst potential consequences and assign the relative values for the assumed severity, occurrence and chance of detection to calculate the risk priority number. Ultimately, the analyst has to develop the recommended action required to reduce the risk associated with potential causes of a failure mode [LN05].

An extension of FMEA called FMECA (Failure Mode, Effects and Criticality Analysis) [FME67] was developed by reliability engineers to evaluate the effect of single component failures. FMECA is adopted and used as a hazard analysis in different domains such as space, nuclear and automotive industries.

2.2.1.3. HAZOP

The Hazard and Operability Study (HAZOP) [Tro68] was initially developed by imperial chemical industries in 1964 and published in 1974. HAZOP is a structured hazard analysis technique to identify risks and operability problems in a given system and develop appropriate safeguards to prevent accidents. HAZOP was originally developed to be used in the chemical industry to identify the potential deviations in chemical processes which can lead to accidents, however, it has been used to identify hazards in different systems in the different domains (e.g. computer systems, software systems) [McD+95]. HAZOP can be applied

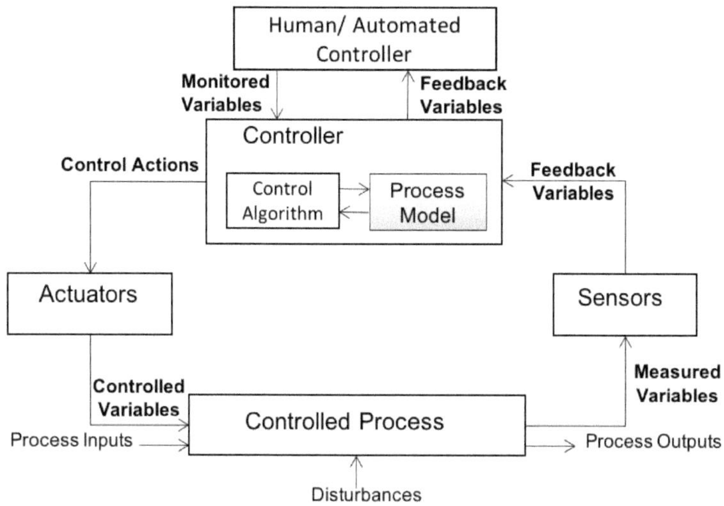

Figure 2.2.: A general feedback control structure

on existing system or during the system design phase before the system has been implemented. The HAZOP process provides guide-words combined with process parameters (e.g. flow, pressure, time, etc.) to help the analysts in identifying possible hazards in a system. These guide-words are used to systematically consider the possible deviations from normal operations of systems like "No", or "more" or "less" or "as well as " or "part of" or "Reverse" or "other than".

2.2.2. System-Theoretic Safety Analysis

The nature of accident causation has, however, become more complex over time. Twenty years ago, accidents causation theory was developed further to capture this increased complexity and a new class of models emerged based on a holistic and systematic approach [Lev04a]. Furthermore, the prevailing chain-of-failure-events models provide the basis for almost all of today's hazard analysis techniques and the probabilistic risk assessment based on them. All of these analysis and design techniques focus on hardware component failures and thus reliability theory [Lev11]. These methods assume that accidents are caused by component failures. However, they are not enough to explain accident causation in the more complex systems.

The development of accident causation models and safety analysis from formerly sequential models to systemic models shows the evolution of safety analysis for complex systems. We must emphasis that traditional analysis types, like FMEA or FTA have been designed for simpler systems than nowadays being created in the industry. The integration of technological, software system components stretches the limits of safety analysis. Therefore, new methods are needed which can actually cope with today's complex systems.

To overcome the limitations of the traditional hazard analysis, a recent countermeasure is to advance safety analysis techniques by system and control theory rather than reliability theory. The STAMP (System-Theoretic Accident Model and Processes) [Lev04a] accident model developed by Leveson, which uses system theory and treats safety as a control problem. Hence, it describes the system as a whole as opposed to linear cause effect relationships or epidemiological factors within the system. STAMP also continues corresponding hazard and accident analysis methods. Within this method, accidents are considered as results from inadequate enforcement of safety constraints in system design, development and operations. STAMP treats safety as a control problem rather than component failures. STAMP is based on system theory, which was designed to understand the structure and behavior of any type of system. In a system-theoretic approach, the system is seen as a set of control components which interact with each other (shown in Figure 2.2). This helps to create models of systems which cover human, technology, software, and environmental factors [Lev04a]. Therefore, STAMP considers accidents not only arising from component failures, but also from the interaction among system components. In other words, accidents occur when component failures, external disturbances and/or dysfunctional interactions among system components are not adequately handled by the safety control system [Lev04a].

The STAMP approach can be divided into two different analysis methodologies. While STAMP acts as an underlying theory, the methods STPA (System-Theoretic Process Analysis) and CAST (Causal Accident Analysis based on STAMP) are to be practically used for safety analysis. STPA is designed for safety analysis in the system development and operation stage; the goal here is to identify hazards existing in the system and providing so-called safety constraints to mitigate those hazards. CAST is designed for accident analysis, the goal here is to identify causal factors, which lead to the accident.

2.2.2.1. STPA

STPA (System-Theoretic Process Analysis) [Lev11] is a safety analysis technique based on the STAMP model of accidents for large and complex systems. STPA has been developed to identify more thoroughly causal factors in complex safety-critical systems including software design errors. STPA aims to create a set of unsafe scenarios that can lead to an accident. It is similar to FTA but STPA includes a broader set of potential scenarios, including those in which no failures occur, but the problems arise due to unsafe and unintended interactions among the system components [Lev11]. STPA provides guidance and a systematic process to identify the potential for inadequate control of the system that could lead to a hazardous state which results from inadequate control or enforcement of the safety constraints.

The basic components in STPA are fundamentals of analysis, safety constraints, unsafe control actions, and control structure diagrams and process models (shown in Figure 2.3). A control structure diagram is made up of basic feedback control loops. An example is shown in Figure 2.2. When put together, they can be used to model the high-level control structure of a particular system. In table 2.1, we itemized the most relevant terms of STPA approach.

Furthermore, STPA was developed also to address increasingly common component interaction accidents which can result from design flaws or unsafe interactions among non-failing (operational) components [Lev11]. It accumulates information about how hazards can occur. This information can then be used to eliminate, reduce, and control hazards in system design, development, manufacturing and operations. The STPA safety analysis process is carried out in three major steps (shown in Figure 2.4):

- STPA Step 0. a: Establish the fundamentals of the analysis (e.g. system description, system-level accidents, system-level hazards, safety and design requirements).

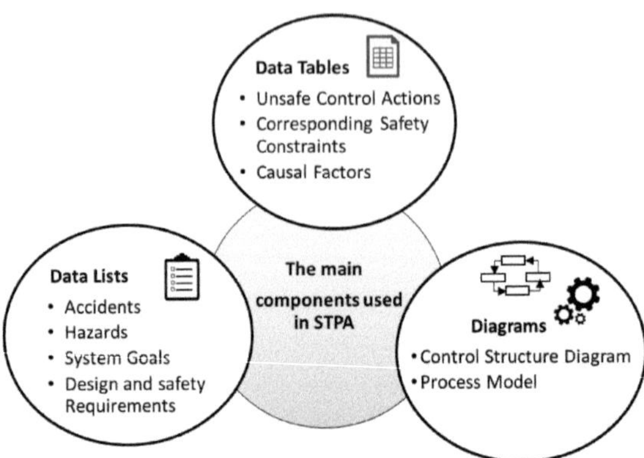

Figure 2.3.: The main components which are used in STPA

- STPA Step 0. b: Draw a high-level safety control structure diagram in which the system is viewed as interacting components. Figure 2.2 shows the general control feedback control structure.
- STPA Step 1: Identify the potential unsafe control actions of the system that could lead to one or more system-level hazards. Leveson [Lev11] defined four types of hazardous actions:
  - A control action required for safety is not provided or is not followed.
  - An unsafe control action is provided that leads to a *Hazard*.
  - A potentially safe control action is provided too late, too early, or out of sequence.
  - A safe control action is stopped too soon or applied too long (for a continuous or nondiscrete control action).
- STPA Step 2: Identify accident scenarios that explain how unsafe control actions might occur and how safe control actions might not be followed or executed.

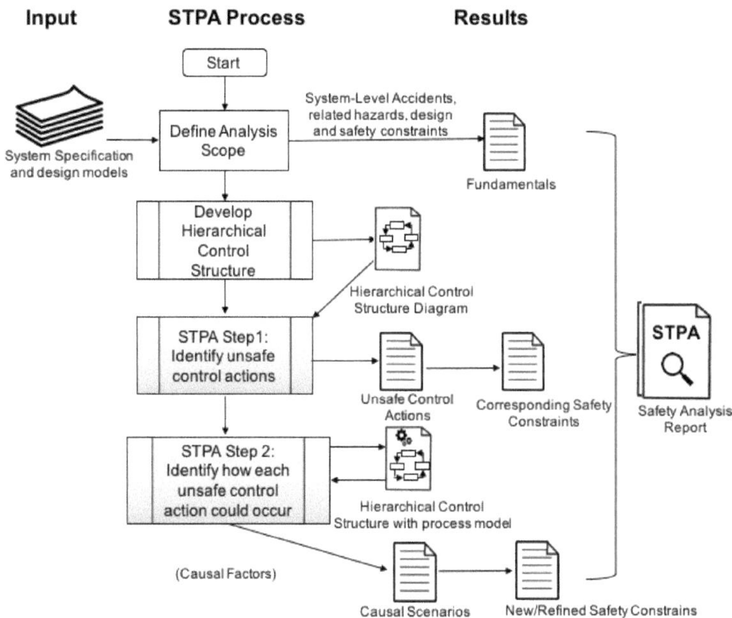

Figure 2.4.: The main steps of the STPA approach

2.2.2.2. Extended Approach to STPA

A new extended approach to STPA was introduced by Thomas [Tho13; TL11], whose approach aims to identify unsafe control actions in STPA Step 1 based on the combination of process model variables of each controller in the control structure diagram. Some control actions in the system can only be hazardous in a certain context. Therefore, the process model variables should be assembled to define a context and analysed based on their context to check whether this combination could lead to a hazard or not. Table 2.2 shows the *Context table* of providing control action CA_i based on the relevant process model variable values $Cs = \bigcup(\mathcal{P}_1 = v_1, \ldots \mathcal{P}_n = v_n)$.

The procedure of the extended approach to STPA is described as follows:

Table 2.1.: STPA Terminology

Terminology	Definition
Accident	Accident (Loss) results from inadequate enforcement of the behavioral safety constraints on the process [Lev11].
Hazard	Hazard is a system state or set of conditions that, together with a particular set of worst-case environmental conditions, will lead to an accident [Lev11].
Unsafe Control Actions	are the hazardous scenarios which might occur in the system due to a provided or not provided control action when it was required. [Lev11].
Safety Constraints	The safety constraints are the safeguards which prevent the system from leading to losses (accidents) [Lev11].
Process model	The process model is a model required to determine the environmental and system variables and states that affect the safety of the control actions and it is updated through various forms of feedback. [Lev11] [Tho13].
Process model variables	The process model variables are the safety-critical variables of the controller in the control structure diagram which have an effect on the safety of issuing the control actions [Lev11] [Tho13].
Causal Factors	Causal factors are the accident scenarios that explain how unsafe control actions might occur and how safe control actions might not be followed or executed [Lev11] [Tho13].

- Identify the relevant process model variables of each control action of the controller in the control structure diagram.
- Create the context table for each control action. A context table is combination sets of the process model variable values (shown in Table 2.2 and Table 2.3).

Table 2.2.: The context table of providing the control action CA_i

Control Action	Process model variables				Hazardous ?		
	P_1	P_2	...	P_n	at any time	too early	too late
CA_i	v_{11}	v_{21}	...	v_{n1}	no/yes	no/yes	no/yes
	v_{12}	v_{22}	...	v_{n2}	no/yes	no/yes	no/yes
	...	...	...	...	..	..	..
	v_{1n}	v_{2n}	...	v_{nn}	no/yes	no/yes	no/yes

Table 2.3.: The context table of not providing the control action CA_i

Control Action	Process model variables				Hazardous ?
	P_1	P_2	...	P_n	
	v_{11}	v_{21}	...	v_{n1}	no/yes
CA_i	v_{12}	v_{22}	...	v_{n2}	no/yes
	...	...	...	...	..
	v_{1n}	v_{2n}	...	v_{nn}	no/yes

- Evaluate each row in the context table (combination set) within two contexts (C_1= **Providing** *CA* or C_2 = **Not Providing** *CA*) to determine whether the control action CA_i is hazardous in that context or not.

Thomas [Tho13] mathematically discussed the formalization of STPA which can be used not only to identify unsafe control actions and other control flaws, but also to generate requirements that will enforce safe behaviors.

2.2.3. Software Safety Analysis Challenges

Safety analysis of software was considered at the beginning of 1970's as a part of the system safety [Eri05]. A number of variations based on the traditional approaches were developed to identify the potential software hazards which may be present to a system such as Software FTA (SFTA), Software FMEA (SFMEA) [FLR78; Rei79]. SFTA (Software Fault Tree Analysis) [LH83a] is an extension of FTA, which is primarily developed to discover all potential faults such as faulty inputs or software bugs that could occur in software. SFTA has also been used for verifying software code. SFMEA (Software Failure Modes and Effect Analysis) [FLR78; Rei79] is an extension of FMEA which was developed in

1978 as a hazard analysis technique for software to address the potential effects of software errors on a system. However, these techniques are insufficient to address software causes and behavior. Leveson stated in [Lev95] that SFTA is applicable only to small-sized software. Because constructing a complete fault tree is not possible for large software.

Leveson (2004) [Lev04b] described the common factors and role of software in spacecraft accidents (e.g. Ariane 5 launcher in 1996, the loss of contact with the solar heliospheric observatory spacecraft in 1998, the loss of the Mars Polar Lander in 1999, and the loss of a Milstar satellite in 1999). Leveson noted that the major root cause of these accidents was arose from flawed requirements and misunderstanding about the associated risks with software during the development process [Lev09]. Leveson also emphasised that the use of software introduces a new causal factor for accidents which involves changes in the traditional hazard analysis techniques (e.g. FTA, FMEA) to consider the software risks.

The assumptions of the accident causes based on the traditional techniques such as FTA and FMEA do not hold for software [Lev09; Lev11]. The software hazard causes in the accident traditional models, are often stated in general terms in hazard analyses called “Software error", instead of defining specifically what software functionality can lead to a catastrophic result [Har10; Har12]. Furthermore, the use of the traditional techniques to identify software hazard is failed when the software might inadvertently activate of a function such as opening a valve at the wrong time or firing a thruster prematurely [Har10; Har12]. Software causes should explicitly describe the software functionality and related system concerns. The term “Software error" does not provide enough information on how the accident occurred. Moreover, software is fundamentally unlike hardware in that software is not hazardous by itself, it has functional failures and does not fail randomly [Eri05; Lev09; Lev95].

In fact, the complexity of software makes defining appropriate software safety requirements by traditional safety analysis techniques difficult. Rather than focusing on creating software safety requirements, most traditional techniques focus on failures and analyse an existing design with some or all of the requirements already defined. Moreover, STPA is a new technique, however, it has not been yet placed within software development process and used for the purpose of software safety.

Table 2.4 shows a summary about the safety analysis techniques: FTA, FMEA, HAZOP and STPA.

Table 2.4.: A summary of the safety analysis techniques

	FTA	FMEA	HAZOP	STPA
Year	1962	1949	1964	2004
Approach	Top-Down	Bottom-up	Bottom-up	Top-Down
Structure	Tree-based	Table-based	Guide words-based	Control loops-based
Theory	Reliability Theory	Reliability Theory	Plants & Process System	System & Control Theory process
Focus	Component failures and human errors	failures of individual components	Event causes of deviations and human errors	Treats safety as control problems
Modeling of System	None	None	None	Control structure diagram of system
Hazard Type	Loss of a component and function or feature	Loss of a component and function or feature	Process errors and human errors	More types of hazards including individual component-related hazards.
Complex System	Difficult	Difficult	Difficult	Cope with complex system
Terminologies	Fault	Failure	potential deviations	Accident (loss) and hazards

2.3. Software Verification

Software verification is a process to check whether software fully satisfies all the expected requirements. Formal verification and testing are two fundamental approaches to software verification. Formal verification techniques are used to prove the correctness of software and check whether the software satisfies its requirements. Three types of formal verification exist: model checking, theorem proving and deductive methods [BK08].

2.3.1. Formal Verification

Formal verification entails a mathematical proof showing that a system satisfies its desired property or specification. To do this, the property of interest must be modeled in a mathematical structure (e.g. temporal logic). Temporal Logic has been proposed by Pnueli [Pnu77] as an appropriate formalism in the specification and verification of concurrent programs. Many different versions of temporal logic have been used in the verification process such as Linear-Time Temporal Logic (LTL), and Computation Tree Logic (CTL) [CE82] which have been broadly used to express safety properties in a formal notation. An LTL formula consists of atomic propositions, Boolean operators ($\neg, \vee, \wedge, \leftrightarrow, \rightarrow, true, false$) and temporal operators ($\bigcirc$ next, $\Box$ always, $\Diamond$ eventually, $\mathcal{U}$ until, $\mathcal{R}$ release). An LTL formula can be expressed by the following syntax [BKL08]:

- If $\beta \in \Psi$ then β is an LTL formula, where Ψ is a finite set of propositional variables which can be used to build the LTL formulas.
- If β and γ are LTL formulas then $\neg\beta$, $\gamma \vee \beta$, $\Box\beta$, $\bigcirc\,\beta$ and $\gamma\,\mathcal{U}\beta$ are LTL formulas.
- If $\Box\beta$, then β is always true for all execution paths.
- If $\Diamond\beta$, then β is true at some time in future states.
- If $\gamma\,\mathcal{U}\,\beta$, then γ is true until β is true.

CTL (Computation Tree Logic) [CE82] is an extension of classical logic proposed by Edmund M. Clarke and E. Allen Emerson in 1981 that allows reasoning about an infinite tree of state transitions. CTL combines both branching-time and linear-time operators. An CTL formula consists of atomic propositions and temporal operations: **A** (All paths), **E** (Exists), **F** (Future), **G** (Globally), **U** (until), **R** (release), **W** (weak until), **X** (next time). The difference between the LTL and CTL formulas is that the LTL formulas are interpreted over a set of linear path of a Kripke structure, whereas the CTL formulas are evaluated over the set of system states [Roz11].

2.3.1.1. Software Model Checking

Model checking is a well-established formal verification technique to verify whether the software meets its requirements through exhaustive exploration of the state space of the software. The model checking process involves that the target software to be formally modelled in the input language of a model checker and specifications/properties to be formalized in a temporal logic such as Linear Temporal Logic (LTL) [Pnu77] or Computation Tree Logic CTL. The model checker will perform an exhaustive exploration to verify whether a given property holds in the software. In case that the software does not hold a given property, a model checker will produce a counterexample that identifies a path where the software violates the given property. There exist two ways to construct or extract the input model required by software model checkers: (1) at the design level, a verification model can be constructed from state machine diagram (e.g. SMV model [McM93]) and (2) at the implementation level, a verification model can be extracted directly from software code (e.g. SPIN model [Hol03]). Model checkers can also be used for testing purposes to generate test cases [ABM98]. In the following, we will describe the most commonly open-source software verification tools:

The Symbolic Model Verifier (SMV) is a model checker which was developed by McMillan [McM93] in 1993 to verify finite state systems against specifications in the Computation Tree Logic (CTL). The SMV language allows to describe the finite state systems. It requires that the given system to be verified is modeled in a suitable model/diagram (e.g. Finite state machines). This model of a given system should be written in the specification language called SMV and the given property (requirement) should be expressed in CTL to check the validity

```
MODULE main (<module variables >)
VAR
variables : <range data type>/<enumeration>
<nameSub1>: _SubModule1 (variables)
...
<nameSubN>: _SubModuleN (variables)
states: <All children states>
ASSIGN
INIT (states=<initialState >)
INIT (<variable> =<value>)
next(<variable >):= case
<var1>=<value> & <tranConditon>:<nextValue >;
...
next(states):= case
<states>=value & transition:nextState;
...
esac;
LTLSPEC
<List of LTL formulae>
CTLSPEC
<List of CTL formulae>
```

Figure 2.5.: The basic structure of the SMV model

of the model against its specifications. The output of the SMV model checker are Boolean values: true or false with a counterexample which shows why the formula does not validate. Figure 2.5 shows the basic structure of the *SMV* model in SMV as described in [McM93; Cav+10]. Each *SMV* module contains the following sections: 1) The name of the model with the optional state variable parameters, 2) The declaration of the state variable and their possible values, 3) The initial values of variables and the *states* variable, 4) The sub-modules of the super module deceleration, 5) The transitions of the module, and a list of the LTL formulae or both.

The NuSMV model checker[1] [Cim+00] is an extension and re-implementation of the symbolic model checker (SMV). NuSMV basically is BDD-based symbolic model checker (Binary Decision Diagram) to verify finite state systems against specifications expressed in LTL. NuSMV provides a textual interaction shell and a graphic interface, extended model partitioning techniques and allows for LTL model checking [Cim+00]. It supports the analysis of specifications expressed in both LTL and CTL.

[1] `http://nusmv.fbk.eu`

Simple Promela Interpreter (SPIN)[1] is an open source software verification tool developed by Holzmann at Bell Labs in 1980[Hol03]. It is used to verify the correctness of distributed software models. SPIN requires that a given system to be verified is described in the specification language called Promela (Process Meta Language) which supports modeling asynchronous distrusted algorithms as non-deterministic finite automaton. Compared to other model checkers, SPIN is a general-purpose model checker which uses an efficient algorithm to reduce the state explosion problem [SK09]. Moreover, SPIN accepts Promela code (verification model) as input which is similar to C code that is written manually or it can be also automatically extracted from source code of software written in ANSI-C by using an extraction verification model tool from implementation level C code such as Modex[2] [HS99].

2.3.1.2. Formal Verification Challenges

Typically, formal software verification focuses on proving the functional correctness of software and demonstrating that the software fully satisfies all functional requirements [Tra+99]. However, they cannot make it safe or reduce the risk. Therefore, the software must be analyzed regarding the safety aspect and verified against its safety requirements at the system level [LCS91]. Formal safety verification involves demonstrating whether the software fulfills its safety requirements and will not result in a hazardous state. The main obstacles to make formal safety verification feasible for large and complex systems are that the formal verification methods needs expert users and the safety requirements are usually written into a natural language. Hence, they cannot be directly verified with model checker [Cim+10]. Therefore, to verify the software against its safety requirements with the model checkers, the safety requirements should be specified into a formal specification in LTL/CTL. For example, a software safety requirement of the train door control system can be written as “the train door software controller must not close the train door when there is a person in

[1]`http://spinroot.com/spin/whatispin.html`
[2]`http://spinroot.com/modex/`

the doorway". This safety requirement can be expressed in an LTL formula as follows:

$LTL_i = \mathrm{G}\ ((person\_in\_the\_doorway\ ) \rightarrow\ !(controlAction = close\_door))$

This formula means that it always (G) the train door software controller must not provide (!) a control action *close_door* when there is a person in the door way.

The main limitation of model checking is the state explosion problem which makes it impossible to scale up and it might be applicable only to finite state programs [AK86]. In some cases, the model checker cannot reach to state in the model and cannot provide an answer. Therefore, the model checker alone is not sufficient to assess the safety of software. The use of formal verification methods can reduce the likelihood of certain software errors or help to detect them, therefore the formal verification methods must complement with appropriate testing[HC12].

2.3.2. Software Testing

Software testing is one of the most important phases during the software development process to detect inconsistencies between the software implementation and its requirements. The complexity of software makes testing a challenging process because practically impossible to test all possible execution paths of software. The main goal of the software testing is to execute a software on a set of test cases and compare the actual results with the expected results. The most common classification of the software testing approaches are black box and white box. Black box testing (functional testing) [Bei95] is a process that tests the functionality of a system under test or software without peering into its internal structure. Whereas white box testing (structural testing) [Pre00] is a process that takes into consideration the internal structure of the system or software under test.

A popular testing approach called Model-based Testing (MBT) [Dal+99; AD97] which is one of the variants of black box testing which aims at automatically generating test cases using models extracted from software requirements. Model-based testing can be performed in three major steps: modelling the system under test, test case generating and test execution. The main challenge of

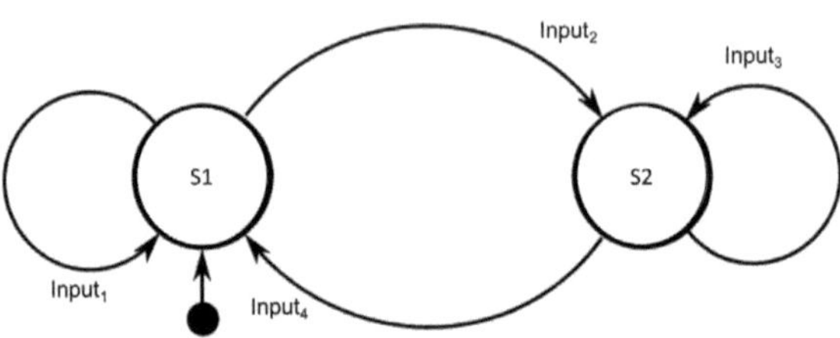

Figure 2.6.: The finite state machine model

software testing is to generate suitable test cases that cover all requirements and functions of the software. The model-based testing process involves creating a suitable model of the software's behavior based on requirements or an existing specification (e.g. finite state machine, extended state machine or statecharts) and generating test data input and expected output to generate the test cases.

2.3.2.1. Software Behavior Models

A number of software behavior models are in use today, several make good models for testing such as control flow charts [Har87], finite state machines [Mea55; Gil62], SpecTRM-RL [Lev00], and sequence event diagrams [UML04]. A software behavior can be described as an input sequence, actions, guards and output logic, or the data flow through the software modules and routines. In the following, we describe popular software behavior models which are used to model software behavior and generate test cases from these models:

Finite state machines are commonly used in software behavior modeling and testing to generate test cases [AD97]. The finite state model (shown in Figure 2.6) includes a set of states, a set of input events and the transition between them.

Definition 2.1 (Finite State Machine (FSM))
Let f be a finite state machine which can be defined with a 5-tuple [Mea55]:

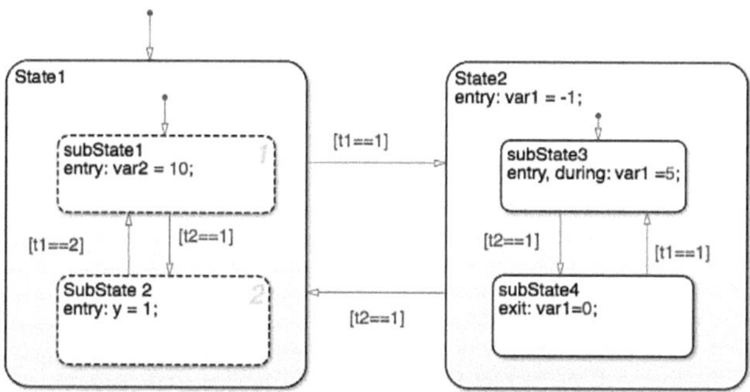

Figure 2.7.: The statechart model

$f = (S, s_1, I, O, T_s)$, where S is a finite nonempty set of states with s_1 as the initial state, I and O are finite input and output alphabets, and T_s is a behavior relation which defines all possible transitions of the finite state machine model.

Another software behavior model is an Extended Finite State Machine (EFSM) which is an extension of the classical (Mealy) Finite State Machine (FSM) model with input and output parameters, context variables, operation and guards defined over context variables and input parameters. EFSM [CK93] is a common and very useful diagram to model the system behavior and suitable for driving the test cases. EFSM contains nodes which represent the states of the system and the directed arcs which represent the transitions of the system from one state to another [UL07].

Definition 2.2 (Extended Finite State Machine (EFSM))
Let M be an extended finite state machine which can be defined by the 7-tuple [CK93]:

$M = (S, I, O, D, F, U, T)$, where S is a set of symbolic states, I is a a set of input symbols, O is the set of output symbols,D is an n-dimensional space $D_1 \times ... \times D_n$, F is a set of enabling function f such that $f_i : D \rightarrow \{0, 1\}$, U is set of update transformations $u_i : D \rightarrow D$, and T is a set of transitions.

Statecharts [Har87] were developed as a broad extension of the conventional formalism of finite state machines with notations of hierarchy, concurrency, and communication for describing the behavior of complex or reactive software systems.

Definition 2.3 (A Statechart)
Let SC be a statechart which can be defined with a 7-tuple [Har87]:

$SC = (S, s_1, \lambda, \xi, \chi, \Omega, \Sigma)$*, where S is a finite set of superstates,* $s_1 \in S$ *is as the start superstate which is a either a state or a state-chart,* λ *is a transition function that maps the set of states S,* ξ *is a superstate function that maps the set of superstates onto itself,* χ *is an event function that maps the set of transitions T,* $S \times S$ *to a set of events,* Ω *is a finite set of events, and* Σ *is a default transition function that maps the set of states S to their default sub-state if it exists, or itself.*

In [Har87] Harel defined the statecharts language and the semantics of statecharts for complex systems. Simply, each Stateflow has a chart which is an independent state machine. Each chart has one or more states which are linked together by arcs labeled with transition information. The states can be also hierarchical states and contain a number of sub-states (children). Each state should have a type of state decomposition *OR_STATE* or *AND_STATE*. The *OR_STATE* decomposition allows only one sub-state (which has a default transition) to be active at a time when the parent (superstate) is active whereas the *AND_STATE* decomposition allows all sub-states to be active when the parent (superstate) is active.

Based on Harel's statechart notations, the Simulink Stateflow model was developed by Mathworks[1] to model event-driven (reactive) systems with enabling the representation of hierarchical state machine diagram, parallelism and history within statechart diagrams. The Simulink Stateflow is generally used to model the discrete controller in the model of a hybrid system where the continuous dynamics such as the behavior of the plant and environment are specified using others capabilities of Simulink toolkit [HR07]. Recently, Matlab/Simulink has become a common model-based development tool for industrial software systems, which is widely used in various industries such as the aircraft, automotive, telecommunications, and transportation industries.

[1] `http://www.mathworks.com`

Figure 2.7 shows an example of the Simulink's Stateflow model. In Simulink's Stateflow, each state can be labeled with the following elements:

name <of a state>

entry: <entry actions are executed when a state is entered.>

during: <during actions are executed when while in a state.>

exit: <exit actions are executed when a state is left.>

entry, during, exit: <combined actions in a state>

The Stateflow model in Fig. 2.7 includes two superstates (state 1 and state 2) with state decomposition *OR_STATE*. The superstate *State 1* has two sub-states with state decomposition *AND_STATE*. When the superstate *State 1* is active, then the both sub-states will be active in the same time. While the superstate *State 2* has two sub-states with state decomposition *OR_STATE*. That means when the superstate *State 2* is active, then only the sub-state with the default transition *subState 3* will be active.

2.3.2.2. Test Case Generation Techniques

A big challenge in software testing is the design of test cases. To generate test cases, the tester needs first to understand the system specification and requirements. After that, the tester has to manually write test cases or automatically generate test cases from a model by using model-based testing tools. Automated generation of test cases involves that the system behavior should be modeled in a suitable model. Over the years, there are many of the automated model-based test case generation approaches which have been developed by different techniques such as random generation algorithms [Pro03], graph search algorithms [Kua62; Bro+05], model-checking [OLA03], symbolic execution [Pre01] or theorem proving [CR02].

2.3.2.3. Combinatorial Software Testing

Today's software systems are complex and their behaviors may be affected by many possible configurations and input variables. Performing exhaustive testing for all possible configurations and input variables of such systems is not always possible for a complex system with a large number of configurations and input variables. For example, if we have a software system with 5 parameters, each of which can take 5 values. Then, the total number of possible combinations of this system is equal to $5^5 = 3125$ possible combinations. Therefore, instead of testing all the possible combinations, combinatorial testing strategies [KKL13] are proposed as reasonable alternative ways that can reduce the number of the possible combinations by generating a subset of combinations to satisfy some of the combinatorial testing coverages. The combinatorial testing is based on the assumption that many errors in software can only arise from the interaction of two or more parameters [KKL13].

Definition 2.4 (Combinatorial Testing)
Combinatorial testing [CG12] is a testing technique that requires covering all t-sized tuples of values out of n parameter attributes or properties modelled after the input parameters or the configuration domain of a system under test.

Two forms of combinatorial testing:1) use combinations of configuration parameter values, or 2) combinations of input parameter values. There are four combination strategy criteria which are used in combinatorial software testing [KKL13]:

- **All Combinations Coverage:** Every possible combination of values of the parameters must be covered.
- **Each Choice Coverage:** Each parameter value must be covered in at least one test case.
- **Pairwise Coverage (2-way):** Given any two parameters, every possible combination of values of these two parameters must be covered in at least one test case.
- **T-way Coverage:** Given any t parameters, every possible combination of values of these t parameters must be covered in at least one test case.

Kuhn et. al [KLK08] show the practical use of combinatorial testing and its feasibility for small to medium-sized modules. They show also the automated generation of tests that provide combinatorial coverage. A tool support for automated combinatorial testing called ACTS[1] was developed by Kuhn at the

[1] `http://csrc.nist.gov/groups/SNS/acts/index.html`

American National Institute of Standards and Technology to generate combination sets of t parameters with n values.

2.3.2.4. Software Safety Testing

Software safety testing [NAS04; Lut00] is a crucial process in developing safety-critical systems to verify whether a software system meets its safety requirements. Safety-critical software should be tested extensively to ensure that the potential software-related hazards have been eliminated or controlled to a low level of risk. The term software safety testing [NAS04] was introduced and implies that software testing should not only address functional requirements, but also the software safety requirements. Therefore, the process for testing safety-critical software combines conventional testing and safety analysis approaches to focus the testing efforts in a specific way to address the safety of the software and test the critical risky situations. In the literature, the software safety testing is also known as "risk-based testing".

The integration between safety analysis and software testing approaches is not trivial. Erdogan et al. (2014) [Erd+14] presented a systematic literature review on the combined use of risk analysis approaches to support testing and testing approaches to support risk analysis. They identified only 32 scientific papers which focus on the combined use of risk analysis and testing with different purposes. The results highlight the value of the combination between risk analysis and testing approaches. Furthermore, the results show that there is a demand for developing more structured and rigorous approaches to use risk-based analysis to support software testing and developing tool support for the combined risk-based testing. Felderer and Schieferdecker (2014) [FS14] presented a taxonomy of risk-based testing and provided a framework to understand and categorize risk-based testing approaches to aid their selection and adoption for specific purposes.

Many existing testing approaches and tools do not incorporate information from safety analysis. Some of them rely on traditional safety analysis such as Fault Tree Analysis (FTA) [Ves+81] and Failure Mode and Effects and Criticality Analysis (FMECA) [FME67] which are grounded in reliability theory and commonly used for the purpose of safety-based testing. However, these approaches focus only on single component failures and they have limitations to cope with complex systems including software. Leveson [Lev11] noted that the primary safety problem in software-intensive systems is not software "failure" but the lack of appropriate constraints on software behavior. The solution is to identify the required constraints and enforce them in the software and overall system design. Thus, STPA [Lev11] was developed to overcome the limitations of the traditional techniques in addressing the unsafe scenarios of complex systems. One of the objectives of this dissertation is to investigate the application of STPA on deriving software safety requirements and develop a novel approach to integrate STPA in the software development process activities, especially the formal verification and testing activities.

Chapter 3

State of the Art

> *Software is hazardous if it can cause other components to become hazardous or it is used to control a hazard.*
>
> — *NASA Software Safety Guidebook*

This chapter provides an overview of the closely related work to this dissertation which has been done in STPA safety analysis, the combined application of safety analysis, formal verification and software testing.

3.1. Generating the Unsafe Control Actions in STPA

Thomas [Tho13] introduced an extended approach to STPA with the purpose of identifying unsafe control actions in STPA Step 1 based on the combination of the process model variables of each controller in the control structure diagram. A combination of process model variables is called a context. Two contexts of control actions are proposed: Provided control action and not provided control action. The control action will be hazardous only in a certain context. The main problem of context tables is the difficulty in defining the combination for a large number of values of the process model variables which have an effect on the safety of control actions. To solve this problem, we [AWL15] developed an algorithm based on the concept of combinatorial testing [KKL13] to automatically generate the context tables and to allow safety analysts to identify a minimal combination of the process model variables and automatically generate the unsafe control actions. The safety analysts can add and apply constraints and Boolean relations to the generated context tables to ignore some unnecessary combinations from these tables. Furthermore, we explain how to automatically refine the unsafe control actions based on the results of the context tables and generate unsafe scenarios for each unsafe control action. The unsafe scenarios will be automatically translated into the refined safety constraints and expressed them into formal specification in LTL. Both algorithms are implemented as an Eclipse plug-in and integrated with XSTAMPP platform.

3.2. Combination of Safety Analysis Techniques and Model Checking

The combination of the safety analysis techniques and model checking for safety verification of complex systems purposes is not something new. There is a number of considerable work has been done in the field of integrating model checkers with traditional safety analysis approaches such as FTA and FMEA. In the following, we discuss the most related work which incorporates the safety analysis and model checking approaches:

Sere and Troubitsyna (1999) [ST99] showed how to formalise the hazard analysis results in a formal system specification, which are semantically different from the specification terms of the controlling software. They used formal methods like the action system formalism [Bac90] (action systems model) which describes parallel programs and reactive programs as a modeling technique of the system behavior and they showed how the results of fault tree analysis (FTA) as a hazard analysis approach can be encoded into the system formalism.

Tribble et al.(2002) [TLM02] proposed a technique for combing traditional safety analysis techniques such as Functional Hazard Analysis (FHA), FTA and FMEA with the formal method approach to conduct a software safety analysis of the flight guidance system requirements model. They used the NuSMV [Cim+00] model checker to verify the safety properties derived from the traditional safety analysis techniques. They also verified some of safety properties with PVS (Prototype Verification System) theorem prover.

Bieber et al. (2002) [BCS02] combined the fault tree analysis and the model checking for safety assessment of complex systems. They designed a language which is called Altarica to model the behavior of systems when faults occur. They used the fault tree analysis to derive the requirements that constraint the design of the system controllers. Then, they used the model checking to assess the designed controller.

Ortmeier et al. (2004) [Ort+04] proposed an integrated approach called $ForMoSA$ which combines safety analysis and formal methods and provides all engineering practices of traditional safety analysis, temporal logic and verification. ForMoSA is built based on fault tree analysis as a safety analysis approach.

Bozzano and Villafiorita (2006) [BV06] presented a safety assessment platform called $FSAP/NuSMV-SA$ based on the NuSMV-SA model checker. The platform integrates the activities of the model design and safety analysis and supports the activities of formal verification. It also supports generating the fault trees and link their top events directly to failure causes.

Recently, Shariva and Papadopoulos (2015) [SP15] proposed an approach that combines the new Symbolic Model Verifier (NuSMV) model checker [Cim+00] with the Hierarchically Performed Hazard Origin and Propagation Studies (HiP-HOPS) safety analysis technique, which automatically constructs fault trees and FMEA from a system model. They showed how such a combination between these approaches can help to verify the design of a system at an early stage in the design phase of a safety critical system. They translated the model of Hip-HOPS into an abstract state machine model. Next, they manually converted the abstract state machine model of a brake-wire system into an SMV Model to be verified by NuSMV. However, its verification is focused on verifying the system Hip-HOPS at the system level.

Most of the above integrated approaches were based on the reliability engineering techniques (e.g. FTA and FMEA) to identify the failure conditions to be verified by model checkers. These approaches aimed at increasing confidence in a software by showing that some classes of errors which are identified by traditional hazard analysis techniques are not present. Even though the model checker shows that the system fulfilled all requirements, that does not necessarily mean the system is safe. In other words, proofing the correctness of system from these errors cannot make it safe and ensure the safety operations of the system.

According to the STAMP accident model assumptions [Lev11], the accidents with systems are caused by software flaws, software specification errors and uncontrolled interaction between different components which form the system rather than failures of a single component [Lev11]. We differentiate our work here from the aforementioned approaches by identifying the STPA-generated unsafe scenarios for each unsafe control action of software controller in the control structure diagram, deriving the detailed software safety requirements at the system level and verifying the software design and implementation against the STPA-generated software safety requirements which constrain the software from these unsafe behaviors. To the best of our knowledge there is no work that integrates STPA safety analysis with software verification. Moreover, we also are not aware of other attempts to automatically transform the software safety requirements derived during safety analysis into formal specifications in LTL.

3.3. Translating Simulink Models into Verification Models

A considerable amount of work has been done on translating Simulink models into models supported by formal verification approaches. In the following, we will discuss the most related work:

Banphawatthanarak et al. [BKB99] developed a tool called *sf2smv* that generates input for the symbolic model checker SMV [McM93] from Stateflow models. In our work, we use the same concept for translating Simulink's Stateflow into the SMV model. As sf2smv is not available yet, however, it is difficult to compare it with our approach in detail.

Meenakshi et al. [MBR06] discussed the principles of translating Simulink models into an input language of a suitable model checker and providing reverse translation of traces violating requirements into Simulink notation for playback. They developed a translator from Simulink to the model checker NuSMV [Cim+00]. The translator takes a Simulink model as input and generates an equivalent NuSMV model. However, this translator is restricted only to discrete Simulink models and support only the basic blocks of Simulink (e.g. logical block or Selector block) that forms the finite state model of a system. Moreover, the translator does not support the translation of Simulink Stateflow into the input language of NuSMV.

Chen and Dong [CD06] proposed a systematic approach to translate Simulink diagrams to Timed Interval Calculus (TIC) [Fid+98], a notation extending Z to support real-time system specification and verification. The translated TIC specification covers the functional and timing aspects of the Simulink blocks. This work aims to guarantee the correctness of control systems. However, this work does not cover Stateflow diagrams.

Chen et al. [Che+12] proposed an approach to systematically translate Stateflow diagrams to into CSP# [Sun+09a]. They developed a translator which is integrated inside the PAT model checker [Sun+09b] to automate the process with support of different Stateflow features. This work aims to validate the functional correctness of Stateflow diagrams by detecting the bugs in the Stateflow model. The properties to be verified are declared in the CSP# model with preprocessor such as *#define*. The translation process preservers the execution semantics of Stateflow and considers advanced Stateflow modelling features such as implicit events and history junctions.

Ferrante et al. [Fer+12] developed a modified tool called Parallel NuSMV (PNuSMV) based on NuSMV model checker [Cim+00] that integrates the ManySAT parallel STA solver [HJS08]. This tool is part of the formal specification verification framework for the formal verification of Simulink/Stateflow models. The tool translates a subset of Simulink blocks (e.g. logical operators and arithmetic blocks) into the NuSMV meta model. The interesting properties are expressed as temporal logic to be verified with the PNuSMV tool. However, this work does not consider translating the Stateflow model into the NuSMV specifications.

We use a similar principle of transforming the Simulink's Stateflow model into an intermediate model with consideration of the state decomposition (AND_STATE and OR_STATE) and the attached actions (Entry, During and Exit). The main contribution of their work, however, is an approach to model check Simulink models which is not our main focus of our approach. Our contribution is to visualise the STPA process model, which is created during the safety analysis, with the Stateflow notation and check its correctness against the STPA software safety requirements. In this way, we ensure that both models contain the same specifications (e.g. names of states, variables and control actions) before using it for generating test cases.

In conclusion, the existing work provide a great basis for our approach but are different in their focus. They concentrate on model checking Simulink models, not the integration with safety analysis or testing. To the best of our knowledge, there is no existing work on constructing the Stateflow diagram based on the information derived during a safety analysis for test case generation.

3.4. Risk-based Software Testing

There are several software safety test techniques in the literature that combine safety analysis principles with model-based testing. Most of them use the term “Risk-based Testing", which combines risk analysis approaches such as FTA, FMECA or Markov chains with software testing approaches (e.g. model-based testing) to create a prioritization criterion for generating test cases.

Redmill [Red04] explored the benefits of risk-based testing as the basis of test planning in the software testing process and how to understand the risks of the system to focus test efforts. He does not show how to generate the test cases from the risk analysis approach.

Zimmermann et al. [Zim+09] proposed a refinement-based approach to the reliability analysis of safety-critical systems. They used statistical testing as a model-based testing technique and a Markov chain model to model the system under test. They also used FTA and FMECA as risk-based analysis techniques to identify the critical situations that represent high risk.

Kloos et al. [KHE11] proposed a model-based testing approach which uses the information derived from FTA in combination with a system model to generate the risk-based test cases. They used FTA to select, generate and prioritize the test cases. They derived the test cases from the combination of fault trees and a basic system behavior model called the “base model".

Our approach uses a similar idea of combining a risk analysis approach with model-based testing. The main difference is that we employ STPA for safety analysis which is based on system and control theory rather than reliability theory like FTA and FMEA. STPA copes with the analysis of complex, modern systems and tackles the dynamic behavior of the system by treating safety as a control problem. Furthermore, STPA provides an abstract model of the system under analysis called the safety control structure diagram which views all main interacting components including the software components of the system. This allows us to directly construct the test model from the control structure diagram and constrain its transitions with the STPA-generated safety requirements.

3.5. Generating Test Cases Using Statechart Diagrams

Over the years, many approaches have been developed to generate test cases from statechart diagrams. The idea behind these approaches is to transform the statechart diagram into an Extended Finite State Machine (EFSM) and generate the test cases from this model. In the following, we will discuss the most related work:

Ural [Ura87] proposed a method to transform the extended finite state machines into a flow graph and generate test sequences. This method is based on the principles of using data flow analysis techniques in software reliability [FO76] to trace the flow graph and generate test cases.

Bourhfir et al. [Bou+97] proposed a unified method for automatic executable test case and test sequences generation which combines both control and data flow testing techniques with control flow criteria (Unique Input Output) and the all-du paths coverage criterion. Their approach generates only executable test cases for EFSM-specified systems by using symbolic evaluation techniques.

Kim et al. [Kim+99] proposed an approach to generate test cases from UML state diagrams based on the conventional control and data flow analysis. The authors have first transformed the state diagrams into EFSM with consideration of the hierarchical and concurrent structure of states (flattened and broadcast) of the UML state diagrams. Then, the EFSM are transformed into the flow graphs. They applied the conventional data flow analysis techniques to the resulting flow graph to generate the test cases. However, they focused only on identifying possible control and data flow and not the values of input variables.

Hong et al. [Hon+00] developed a method for the selection of test sequences from statecharts. The method is based on the STATEMATE semantics of statecharts by Harel [HN96]. The basic idea is to transform the statechart into an EFSM which contains all the possible runs of the statechart. The authors have considered the input variables in the EFSM which was generated from the state machine diagram. The resulting EFSM model will then be transformed into a flow graph to generate test sequences that cover all associations between definitions and uses of each variable that appear in the original state machine. The authors used the existing method of Ural [Ura87] to transform the EFSM into a flow graph that models the flow of both the control and the data in the statechart.

In conclusion, our approach uses a similar principle of generating test cases from the test model by using graph search algorithms (depth-first search, breadth-first search and both combined) which are presented in the aforementioned mentioned approaches. However, we choose different test coverage criterion to generate test cases such as all states coverage, all transition conditions coverage and the STPA software safety requirements coverage. However, our approach transforms each state in the safe test model as an executable Java script function that takes the state variables which are declared in the state actions (Entry, During, Exit) as parameters and execute their equations to update their values. The updated values of these variables will be used to check the transition condition and determine the next state. Moreover, our approach provides traceability between the software safety requirements and test model and traceability between the software safety requirements and the generated test cases.

3.6. Generating Test Cases from Simulink Models

Few research has concentrated on the subject of the automatic generation of test cases from Simulink Stateflow: Zhan and Clark [ZC08] developed an approach for automatic testing of Matlab/Simulink models. Their approach is a search-based test data generation and selection approach. It uses the first search-based approach to generate test data.

Pâsâranu et al. [Pas+09] proposed a framework for model-based analysis and test case generation for flight software of a NASA flight mission based on the Simulink Stateflow and UML representations. They used Java path finder[1] and symbolic path finder[2] to generate test cases from both UML and Simulink/Stateflow models. The proposed framework is based on the concept of using model checking to generate test cases. The framework takes the models which are created by using different modelling environment and enables their analysis with model checking and test case generation approaches.

[1]http://javapathfinder.sourceforge.net

[2]http://babelfish.arc.nasa.gov/trac/jpf/wiki/projects/jpf-symbc

Windisch [Win09] proposed an automation approach for search-based testing of continuous functional models like Simulink Stateflow models. The method demonstrates how search-based testing techniques can be applied to a continuous functional model such as Simulink/Stateflow to generate test cases.

Li and Kumar [LK12] proposed an automatic method for test data generation for Simulink Stateflow based on its translation to input/output extended finite automata model. The method involves that the Simulink Stateflow shall translate to an input/output extended finite automate model. Each path in Input/output extended finite automate model represents a computation sequence of the Simulink Stateflow diagram. They implemented the proposed method by using two model checking techniques and constraint solving. The NuSMV model checker is used to map the input/output of the extended finite automata to a finite abstracted transition system modeled in SMV and generate test cases by checking each path in the I/O of the extended finite automata against the resultant model.

We differentiate our work here from the aforementioned approaches by automatically generating the safe test model from the Stateflow model which is constructed from the safety analysis specification. Our approach also shows how to validate the correctness of the safe test model against the software safety requirements by using the NuSMV model checker.

CHAPTER 4

APPROACH

> *Safety is a system property and software, of itself, cannot be safe or unsafe.*
>
> — JOHN MCDERMID

This chapter introduces the proposed approach for safety engineering of software-intensive systems based on STPA, called *STPA SwISs*. The content of this chapter has been presented and published in the paper at the 33rd International Conference, SAEFCOMP 2014 Workshop [AW14b], the paper at the 34th International Conference, SAFECOMP 2015 [AW15a] and the paper at the 3rd European STAMP Workshop, Procedia Engineering Journal [AWL15].

Developing safety-critical software requires a more systematic software and safety engineering process that enables the software and safety engineers to recognize the potential software risks. For this purpose, we propose a system-theoretic safety engineering approach based on STPA including software verification activities [AWL15]. The proposed approach is abbreviated as STPA SwISs (STPA-based Approach for Software-Intensive Systems) which provides seamless safety and verification activities to allow the software and safety engineers to work together during the software development for safety-critical systems. STPA SwISs provides a concept of applying STPA to software components at the system level to identify potentially unsafe control actions and to derive the corresponding software safety requirements that prevent software system to transition into a hazardous state. Furthermore, STPA SwISs provides an algorithm to automatically transform the software safety requirements into formal specifications in Linear Temporal Logic (LTL) [Pnu77] to facilities the verification activities of software design and implementation with the model checker against the STPA results. In addition, STPA SwISs provides a concept

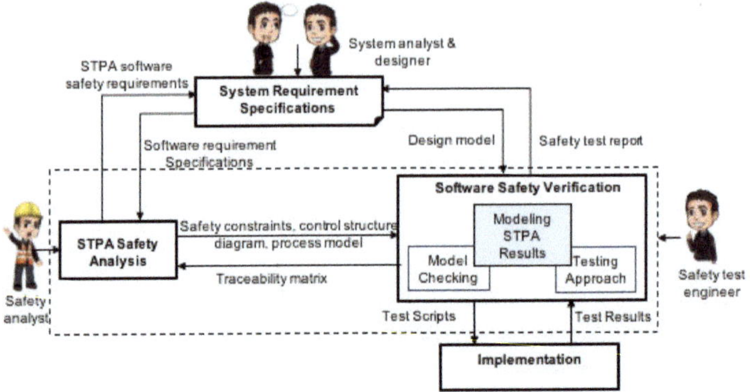

Figure 4.1.: STPA SwISs- A Safety Engineering Approach for Software-Intensive Systems

of automatically generating safety-based test cases from information derived during STPA safety analysis to test the software system against the STPA results.

The *STPA SwISs* approach can be applied during the development process of new software or to existing software and defines the following roles (shown in Figure 4.1):

- **Safety analyst** will apply STPA and derive the software safety requirements at the system level.
- **System analyst and designer** will model the system specification and model the results of STPA in a suitable model (e.g. Simulink Stateflow).
- **Safety tester** will verify the constructed model against the STPA-generated software safety requirements and generate the safety-based test cases. The key idea here is to use two verification approaches (i.e. model checking and testing approach) to provide a sufficient evidence that the software is safe to operate. The safety tester will use the model checking to verify the software against its STPA-generated safety requirements and check the correctness of the test model. Safety tester also will use the testing approach to generate safety-based test cases for each software safety requirement. The STPA SwISs approach uses both software verification

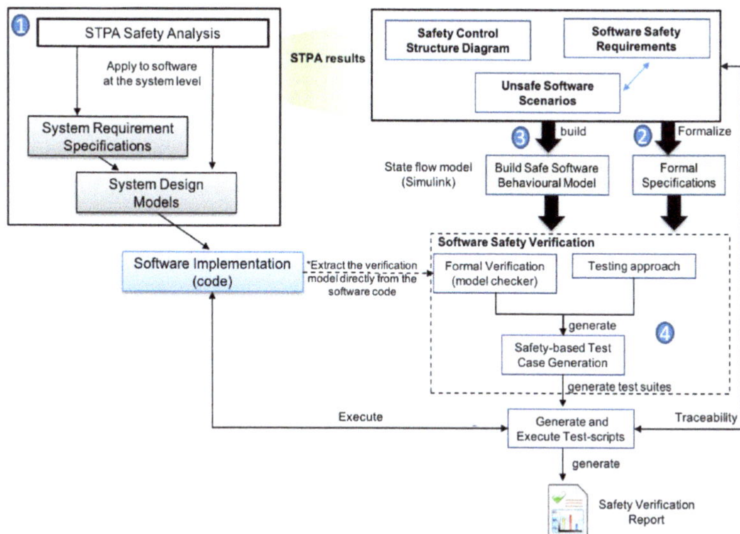

Figure 4.2.: Detailed STPA SwISs approach

approaches (formal verification and testing) to focus the testing efforts in a specific way to address the safety of the software. This, in turn, shall help the software and safety engineers to test the critical risky situations and provide a proof that the software satisfies its STPA-generated safety requirements.

The STPA SwISs approach is carried out in four major steps (shown in Figure 4.2: 1) deriving the software safety requirements of a software controller at the system level, automatically generating the unsafe scenarios based on the extended approach to STPA by Thomas [Tho13], and automatically expressing the STPA-generated safety requirements in formal specifications in LTL; 2) constructing the safe behavioral model of the software controller with the statechart notations in Simulink. A safe behavioral model is a statechart notation that models the process model variables of a software controller in the STPA control structure diagram as states and the control actions as the state actions, and it is

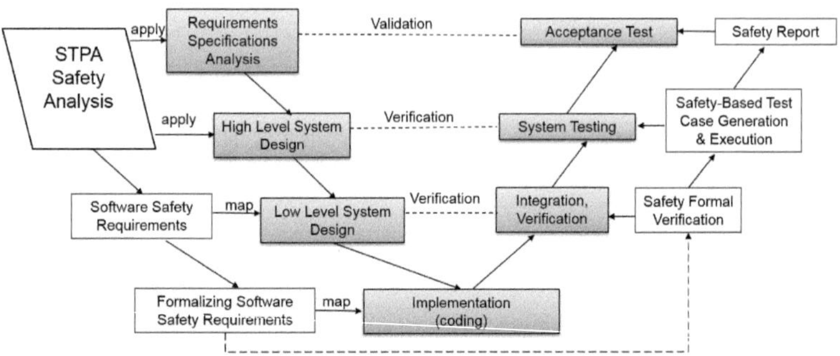

Figure 4.3.: STPA SwISs activities during the V-Model development process

constrained by the STPA-generated software safety requirements (transitions); 3) transforming the safe behavioral model into an input model of the NuSMV model checker and checking the correctness of the generated model against the STPA and safety requirements expressed in LTL; and 4) automatically generating a safety-based test model and deriving the safety-based test cases from this model.

Figure 4.3 shows the STPA SwISs activities during the development process of the new software. The initial input of safety engineering is the system specification and requirements. Based on these specifications, the safety analyst will perform the STPA safety analysis, which is the starting point of the safety engineering process. In the following sections we describe in more detail the five major activities:

4.1. Deriving Software Safety Requirements

This step starts by applying STPA to the system specification to identify STPA software safety requirements and the potentially unsafe scenarios which the software can contribute to. The algorithm starts by establishing the fundamentals of analysis by determining the system-level accidents (*ACC*) and the associated system-level hazards (*HA*) which the software can lead to or contribute in. Next, the algorithm demands that the safety control structure diagram of the system shall be constructed from the system specifications. The software here is the controller in the control structure diagram.

Definition 4.1 (A Control Structure Diagram)
The Control Structure Diagram (CSD) of a software system can be expressed with five-tuples (CO, AC, SO, CP, CA), where CO is a set (one or more) of the software controllers which control the controlled processes (CP) by issuing control actions to the actuators, AC is a set of the actuators which implement the control actions (CA) of the controller, CP is a set of the controlled processes which are controlled by controllers (CO). SO is a set of sensors which send the feedback about the status of the controlled process.

Each controller in the control structure diagram must contain a model of the assumed state of the controlled process, called the process model [Lev11]. A process model contains one or more variables, the required relationships among the variables, the current state and the logic of how the process can change state. This model is used to determine what control actions are needed. It is updated through various forms of feedback [Lev11]. The process model is a part of the internal state of the controller in the control structure diagram.

Definition 4.2 (A Software Controller)
A software controller CO_i can be expressed formally as a two-tuple $CO_i = (CA, PM)$, where CA is set of the control actions and PM is the process model of the controller which has a set of process model variables (PMV), which are a set of critical variables P and states S that have an effect on the safety of CA: $P = \bigcup(\mathcal{P}_1 = v_1 \ldots \mathcal{P}_n = v_n)$, where P_1 and P_n are process model variables of the software controller CO_i with their values v_1 and v_n.

We classified the process model variables of the software controller that affect the safety of the critical control actions into three types: 1) *Internal variables* which change the status of the software controller, 2) *Interaction interface variables* which receive and store the data/command/feedback from the other components in the system, and 3) *Environmental variables* of the environmental components that interact with or are controlled by the software controller.

The safety analyst can derive the software safety requirements for each software controller in the control structure diagram by performing the following steps:

1. STPA Step 1: Identify unsafe control actions. In this step, the safety analyst will identify the potentially unsafe software control actions for each software component that can lead to one or more of the defined system hazard *HA*, as follows:
   a) Identify all safety-critical Control Actions (*CAs*) that can lead to one or more of the associated hazards (*HA*).
   b) Evaluate each CA with four general types of hazardous behaviors to identify the Unsafe Control Actions (*UCAs*): (a) a control action required for safety is not provided, (b) an unsafe action is provided, (c) a potentially safe control action is provided too early, too late or out of sequence and (d) a safe control action is stopped too soon or continued too long.
   c) Translate the identified *UCAs* manually into informal textual Software Safety Requirements (*SSR*).
   d) Identify the process model and its variables and include them in the software controller in the control structure diagram to understand how each *UCA* could occur. The process model describes the states of the software controller (only critical states which are relevant to the safety of the control actions) and their variables describe the software communication, input and output.
   e) Automatically generate the critical set of combinations of the process model variables for each control action (*CA*). Each combination should be evaluated within two contexts (C_1= **Providing** *CA* or C_2 = **Not Providing** *CA*) to determine whether the control action is hazardous in that context or not. A control action *CA* could be considered hazardous in context C if only a combination of process variables related to *CA* leads to a system-level hazard $H \in HA$. The context C_1 = **Providing** *CA* has three types of sub-contexts: *context*

incorrectness, in which the unsafe control action commanded incorrectly and caused a hazard (any time), *context real-time execution*, in which the unsafe control action commanded in a wrong timing (too early or too late) or sequence, and *context execution mechanism*, in which the unsafe control action commanded in a wrong mechanism of execution (applied too long or stopped too soon).

2. STPA Step 2: Identify the unsafe software scenarios for each unsafe control action. Based on the results of STPA Step 1, the safety analyst will identify the unsafe software scenarios for each unsafe control action *UCA* as follows:
   a) Identify the potentially unsafe critical combination of unsafe software control actions and evaluate it to identify the potential unsafe scenarios of the software controller that cause accidents.
   b) Refine software safety requirements based on the unsafe scenarios of the software controller.

The output of this step is a safety control structure diagram with a process model, a list of software safety requirements, and a set of unsafe software scenarios, and a list of the refined software safety requirements and refined unsafe control actions.

4.2. Formalising Software Safety Requirements

Once the corresponding software safety requirements have been identified and expressed by Boolean operators, these requirements can be easily mapped into a formal specification in LTL to be able to verify them by model checking. A safety requirement (property) ensures something bad (hazardous behavior) never happens during the execution. The safety tester has to transform the STPA-generated safety requirements into formal specification in LTL [AW15a].

Definition 4.3 (LTL formula)
Let $RSSR_i$ be a software safety requirement which must always be true for all execution paths of a software. Then an LTL formula φ of $RSSR_i$ can be expressed as follows:

$$LTL_i = \Box(RSSR_i), where\ RSSR_i = (Cs = \bigcup(\mathcal{P}_1 = v_1, \dots \mathcal{P}_n = v_n) \rightarrow (CA_i)) \vee RSSR_i = (Cs = \bigcup(\mathcal{P}_1 = v_1, \dots \mathcal{P}_n = v_n) \rightarrow (\neg\, CA_i))$$

This formula means: The occurrence of $Cs = \bigcup(\mathcal{P}_1 = v_1, \dots \mathcal{P}_n = v_n)$ always implies ($\rightarrow$), that the software must (or mustn't) provide the control action CA_i. Based on the above definitions, the software safety requirements identified by safety analysis activities can be easily translated into LTL. This step can be fully automated by converting Boolean expressions of the hazardous combinations of process model variables into LTL. The LTL formulae will be also transformed into CTL formulae with CTL operators to support the verification activities with CTL.

4.3. Constructing a Safe Software Behavioral Model

To verify the software design against the results of STPA and generate the corresponding safety-based test cases directly from the information derived from the STPA safety analysis, each software controller's behavior in the control structure diagram must be modelled in a suitable behavioral model and constrained by the STPA safety requirements. For this purpose, the system designer and safety analyst should work together to construct a safe behavioral model of each software controller based on the system specification and the safety control structure diagram that contains the process model of the software controller. The safe behavioral model should be labeled with software safety requirements as derived by STPA. A safe behavioral model explores the safe behaviors of the software controller based on the results of STPA. It includes only the process model variables that affect the safety of control actions of the software controller, their relationship, and the ways in which the system can migrate from one state to another (shown in Figure 4.4). For this purpose, we select the Stateflow [Mat16] diagram notations to visualize the automation model of each software controller. The Stateflow diagram is a visual notation for describing dynamic behavior, including the hierarchy, concurrency and communication information. The idea here is to build a model from STPA results with a modeling editor (e.g. Simulink) that supports the export of the statechart notations as XML specifications.

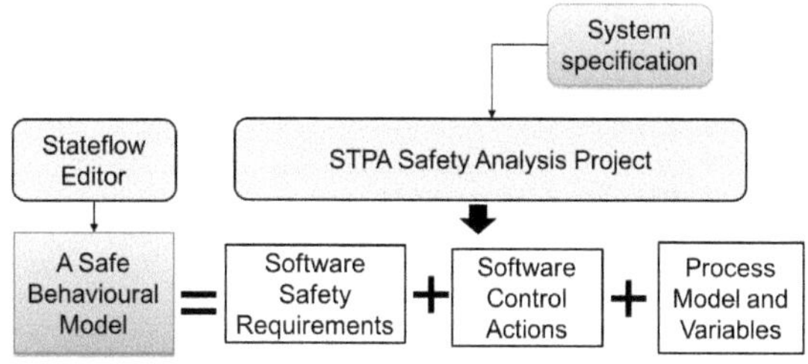

Figure 4.4.: A safe software behavioral model

Definition 4.4 (Safe Behavioral Model (SBM))
Let SBM *be a Safe Behavioral Model (shown in Fig. 4.4) which can be expressed by a three-tuple (PMV, T, CA), where* PMV *is a set of the safety-critical process model variables: critical variables P and S states: P ⊂ PMV and states S ⊂* PMV*, T is the set of transition conditions which are extracted from the STPA refined software safety requirements* RSSR *that are refined based on* PMV*, and* CA *is the set of the critical software control actions.*

Each transition T_i of the safe behavioral model is expressed with the syntax $T_i = IE\ [SSR]\ /\ TA$, where *IE* is the input event that causes the transition T_i, *SSR* is a safety requirement which is a Boolean condition that constraints the transformation from the current state to the next state, and *TA* is an action that will be executed when the Boolean expression is valid. Each state in the Stateflow model has three optional types of actions: *Entry, During and Exit* actions. Entry actions execute when the state is entered, *During* actions execute when the state is active, an event occurs and no valid transition to another state is available, and *Exit* actions execute when the state is active and a transition out of the state occurs [Mat16]. These actions are used to determine how to change the current state of the software controller to the next state.

The syntax of the Stateflow in Simulink allows to combine these three actions that execute the same tasks in a state. To change values of the process model variables $P = \bigcup(\mathcal{P}_1 = v_1 \wedge \ldots \mathcal{P}_n = v_n)$ in a state, we used these actions of each state in the safe behavioral model to determine how each value of the process

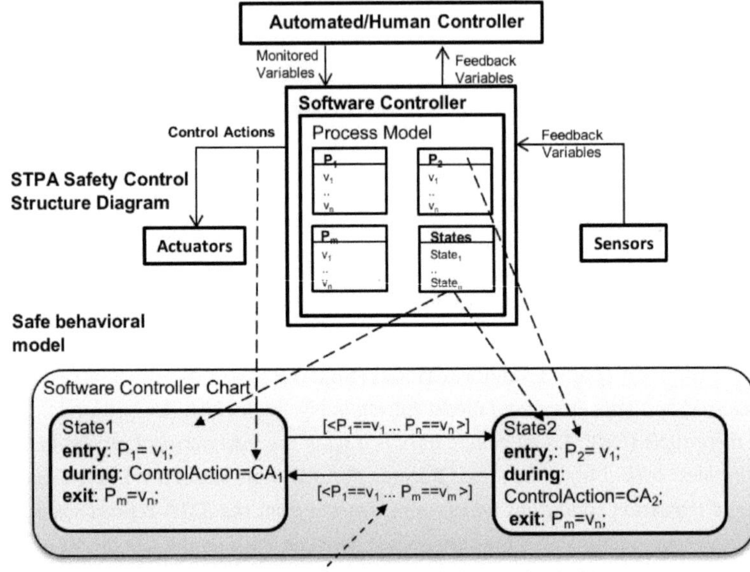

Figure 4.5.: Mapping the process model variables and control actions into the safe software behavioral model

model variable (P_i) can be changed when the software controller enters or exists or this state. For example, the process model variable P_i in the process model of the software controller can be written in a state as an Entry, During or Exit action or combined state actions as follows: $entry, during, exit$: P_i = *<new value of* P_i *>*.

As the transition condition is derived from the refined STPA software safety constraints, the new value of each process model variable will be used to check the transition condition of the current state to determine what is the next state. We also used these state actions to determine which control action of the software controller can be dispatched on entering, during or exiting the current state. Figure 4.5 shows how to map the internal process model variables of the software controller and its control actions into the safe behavioral model. We identify the rules of constructing a safe software behavioral model from the STPA results as follows:

- The safe behavioral model should contain all internal state process variables of the software controller in the STPA control structure diagram: $PMV \subset S \in SBM$, where S is a set of software controller states.
- All process model variables of the software controller in the STPA control structure diagram should be declared in the safe behavioral model.
- The safe behavioral model should constrain the transitions using the STPA software safety requirements (constraints) which are identified based on the rules 3 and 4.
- Define an enumeration data type variable named *controlAction* in the safe behavioral model which takes all control actions of the software controller in the STPA control structure diagram as its value.
- The *controlAction* variable will be used as an entry action of internal states of the safe behavioral model to show which control action will be issued when the software controller enters a state.

4.4. Software Safety Verification

This step aims at verifying the STPA software safety requirements based on the verification model which is constructed from the safe behavioral model at the design level or extracted directly from the source code at the implementation level. It aims also to validate the correctness of the safe behavioral model to check whether it violates its STPA safety requirements. The input of this step is the safe behavioral model and the STPA results. The safety test engineer should perform the verification activities in this step with two complementary tasks: (1) formal verification and (2) testing.

The safety test engineer should perform the software formal verification through the following two sub-tasks:

- Extracting the input verification model of the model checker. The verification model can be constructed in two ways: (a) construct the verification model from the safe behavioral model into the SMV model at the design level. In this case, the verification model will be verified by using the NuSMV model checker, or (b) Extract the verification model directly from the software code by using the extraction the verification model tools such as Modex [HS99] for ANSI-C Code at the implementation level. In this case, the verification model will be verified by using the SPIN model checker, and

- Verifying the verification model against each the STPA-generated software safety requirement specified in the LTL to ensure that the verification model of the software controller satisfies the STPA safety requirements. When the verification model violates any STPA-generated software safety requirement during the execution of the verification procedure, a counterexample will be produced. A counterexample contains information where the software does not meet these constraints (e.g. software states, initial state and variables and their values). The verification of the software controller can be performed at the design level or after finishing the implementation of software controller.

4.5. Safety-based Test Case Generation

Safety-based testing is a process to generate automatically test cases based on a given model which is constructed from the information derived during safety analysis. The safe behavioral model will be used as input to the safety-based testing process to generate safety-based test cases. The safety test engineer should perform the safety-based testing process through the following four sub-tasks:

- Automatically convert the safe behavioral model of the software controller into the input model of the safety-based testing tool which we developed.
- Select suitable test coverage criteria (i.e. all transactions coverage, all state coverage, or action coverage) to ensure that every transaction in the safe behavioral model is considered.
- Set the input test data for the critical variables of the software system under test, and

- Use the safety-based testing tool to perform the traversal on the safe behavioral model. During traversal, collect the actions, conditional expressions (i.e. guards) and test input and output data on each transition to generate safety-based test cases.

The output of this step is the safety-based test cases to be grouped into test suites. A test suite comprises a group of relevant test cases. The model checking is used here to verify the safe behavioral model against the results of STPA to ensure that the safe model includes and satisfies the STPA results. It is also used to generate specific test cases for each software safety requirement.

4.6. Summary

We presented a comprehensive safety engineering approach that integrates the modern safety analysis approach STPA with software verification approaches (formal verification and testing) to enable safety engineers to verify the software against the software safety requirements which are derived at the system level. The proposed approach exploits the advantages of applying STPA to software at the system level to identify potentially unsafe scenarios of software and derive the software safety requirements that prevent software to provide unsafe control action. The approach also exploits the benefits of the software verification approaches to directly verify the software design and implementation against its software safety requirements. One of the key benefits of the proposed methodology is that it can be iterated until the software meets all software safety requirements.

The limitation of the proposed approach is that there are still manual interventions required to be performed by safety test engineers in constructing the safe behavioral model. Another limitation is mapping the specifications of the STPA safety analysis (e.g. process model variables and safety constraints) into the safety behavioral model specifications (e.g. states, input variables and transition conditions). Therefore, we provided two ways to check the correctness of the safe behavioral model before using it in the test cases generation: 1) The tool support allows the safety test engineers to manually check the validation of the safe behavioral model by providing a validation user interface which shows both

STPA and safe behavioral model specifications in one table, and 2) automatically transform the safe behavioral model into an SMV model and use the NuSMV model checker to verify it against the STPA safety requirements specified in LTL.

As it is known, manual construction of the formal specification of the safety requirements may lead to huge effort and time. Therefore, we developed an algorithm to automatically generate the LTL formulae of each safety requirements and check its consistency. Furthermore, the formal verification methods (e.g. model checker) still do not scale up well, difficult in practices and need user expertise. Therefore, we provided a high degree of automation to support the main steps of the proposed approach to facilitate a seamless use of the safety analysis and software safety verification activities by little or no prior experience.

CHAPTER 5

AUTOMATION OF APPROACH

> *When the ideas are coming, I don't stop until the ideas stop because that train doesn't come along all the time.*
>
> — *DR. DRE*

In this chapter, we describe the algorithms to automate some activities of the *STPA SwISs* approach to help the software and safety engineers to derive the software safety requirements, automatically formalise them in LTL, verify them and generate safety-based test cases. Figure 5.1 shows the automation process of the STPA SwISs approach.

5.1. STPA Components in XML Specification

The STPA approach has different data components which are used to document the analysis results (as shown in Figure 2.3) such as:1) Data lists (e.g. accident lists, hazard list, system goals, safety and design requirements); 2) Diagrams (e.g. hierarchical and detailed safety control structure diagram and process model); and 3) Data tables (e.g. unsafe control actions table, causal factors tables and corresponding safety constraints table). To facilitate the implementation of the STPA process, we first provide an internal representation of each STPA component in XML (Extensible Markup Language) specification. Each STPA component is associated with an XML element that documents the input data (shown in Figure 5.2). Each STPA component has a unique Id and name.

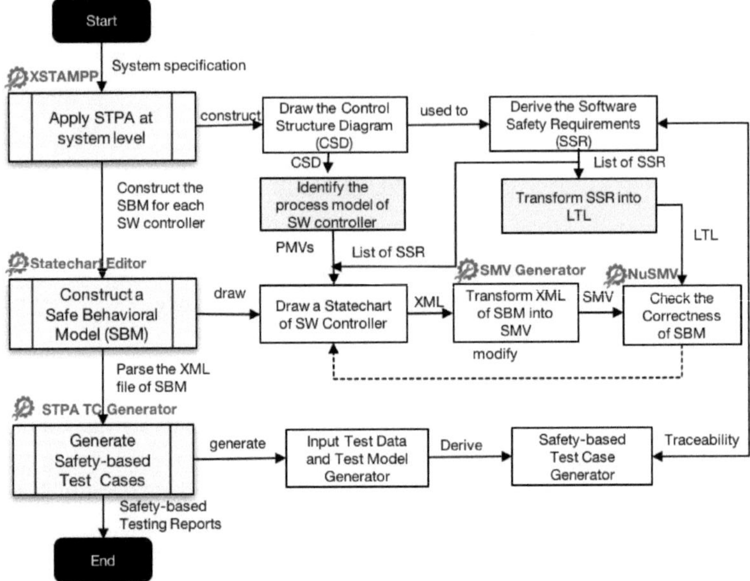

Figure 5.1.: The detailed automation support of the STPA SwISs approach

5.2. Automatically Generate Unsafe Scenarios

In this section, we explain how to automatically generate the context table based on the process model variables of the software controller and how to automatically generate the unsafe scenarios. Furthermore, we show how to generate a minimal combination set of process model variables for a software controller with a large number of the process model variables by using the combinatorial testing algorithm [KKL13].

5.2.1. Generate Context Tables

Traditionally, the STPA-generated safety requirements are written in natural language. In the following, we show how to automatically refined the STPA-generated safety requirements and transform them into formal specification

```xml
<?xml version="1.0" encoding="UTF-8" standalone="yes"?>
<ns2:dataModelController astpaversion="2.0.6" xmlns:ns2="astpa.model">
<projectdata>
<styleRanges/>
<projectDescription>...</projectDescription>
<projectName>...</projectName>
</projectdata>
<accidents/>
<hazards/>
<links/>
<safetyConstraints/>
<systemGoals/>
<designRequirements/>
<controlstructure>
<component><id> </id> <text></text>
<isSafetyCritical>false</isSafetyCritical>
<componentType>ROOT</componentType>
<children>
<controllers/>
<actuators/>
<controlledProcess/>
<sensors>
<controlactions/>
<processModel>
<processvariable><processvalue> </processvalue> </processvariable>
</processModel>
</children>
<unsafecontrolactions/>
<crossroadingsafetyconstraints/>
<causalFactors/>
</ns2:dataModelController>
```

Figure 5.2.: The XML specifications of STPA components

in LTL. To refine the informal textual software safety requirements which are derived in STPA Step 1, the safety analyst has to identify the process model of each software controller and its critical variables which have an effect on the safety of control actions. For each control action in the control structure diagram, the critical combinations (context tables) can be generated based on the following definition:

Definition 5.1 (Context Table)

Let CA_i is a control action which is commended by a software controller CO_i to an actuator AC_i, and $PMV = \bigcup(\mathcal{P}_1 \ldots \mathcal{P}_n)$ is a set of the process model variables that *have an effect on the safety of the control action CA_i. Each process model variable P_i has V_i values. Then, the context table C can be generated based on the following equation: $C_{CA} = |P_1| \cdot |P_2| \ldots |P_i| = |P_1 \times P_2 \times \ldots \times P_n| = |\prod_{i=1}^{n} P_i|$, where $\times$ is the Cartesian product operator, i is the number of process model variable and n is the total number of process model variables.*

The context table is the results of the Cartesian product between the values of the process model variables. Based on the generated combination sets Cs, the safety analyst has to evaluate each control action in two contexts *Providing* and *Not Providing*.

5.2.1.1. Identify a Minimal Combination of Process Model Variables

The main problem of automatically generate the context tables is the difficulty in defining the combination for a large number of values of the process model variables which have an effect on the safety of control actions. To solve this problem, we developed an algorithm based on the concept of combinatorial testing [KKL13] to automatically generate the context tables and allow safety analyst to identify a minimal combination of process model variables by adding constraints and Boolean relations on the generated context tables to ignore some unnecessary combinations from these tables.

5.2.1.2. Generate the Unsafe Scenarios

Each item in the context table will be evaluated manually by the safety analyst. If a critical combination set is hazardous in the context of providing or not providing the control action CA_i, then a hazardous rule will be automatically generated based on the combination set.

Definition 5.2 (Refined Unsafe Control Action)
The refined unsafe control action (RUCA) is a four-tuple (CA, Cs, C, TC), where CA is a control action which causes a hazard H ∈ HA, $Cs = \bigcup(\mathcal{P}_1 = v_1, \ldots \mathcal{P}_n = v_n)$ which is a critical set of combinations of the relevant process model variables PMV of CA, C is a context where providing or not providing the control action CA is hazardous, and TC is the type of context ***providing*** *of control action CA (****any time, too early*** *or* ***too late****).*

Algorithms 5.1 Algorithm of generating context tables and transform safety software requirements into LTL specification

Input: *CAs* : A list of control actions, $PMV_{i,j}$: A table of process model variables $\bigcup\mathcal{P}$ and values
Data: C : Two contexts {Provided, Not Provided}
Output: LTL= A list of LTL specifications
Description:

for each control action $CA_i \in CAs$ **do**
  for each context $C_i \in C$ **do**
    Define a dependency matrix $D_i = CA_i \times PMV$
  end for
  Construct an input text file N_i with ACTS plug-in format
  $ACTS \leftarrow N_i$
  Generate combination sets $CS_i = \bigcup(\mathcal{P}_{i,1} \wedge \ldots \mathcal{P}_{i,n})$
  Evaluate each combination set $f(\overrightarrow{CS_i})$
  if $f(\overrightarrow{CS_i})$ is **hazardous** in the context C_i **then**
    Check for any conflicted combination set in CS
    if $f(\overrightarrow{CS_i})$ is not **conflicted then**
      Refined Safety Requirements $\overrightarrow{SR_i}$
      $\overrightarrow{SR_i} = (\Omega CS_i \rightarrow (CA_i \vee \neg CA_i))$
      $LTL_i \leftarrow G(SR_i)$
    end if
  end if
end for

To automatically translate each critical combination of process model variables for each control action *CA* into the unsafe software scenarios, we set the following rules:

Rule 1: Each refined unsafe control action (*RUCA*) in the context of **Providing** (C_1) of a control action CA_i can be expressed as:

$RUCA_i$ = <CA> **provided** <TC> **is hazardous when** <Cs= $\bigcup(\mathcal{P}_1 = v_1, \ldots \mathcal{P}_n = v_n)$> occurred.

Rule 2: Each refined unsafe control action (RUCA) in the context of **Not Providing** (C_2) of a control action CA_i can be expressed as:

$RUCA_i$ = <CA> **Not provided is hazardous when** <Cs= $\bigcup(\mathcal{P}_1 = v_1, \ldots \mathcal{P}_n = v_n)$> occurred.

By using the rules 1 and 2, we refine the unsafe control actions which are identified based on the combination set of process model variables. The software safety requirements are generated automatically from the refined unsafe control actions. Based on definition 3, we identify the following rules which are used to automatically generate the Refined Software Safety Requirements ($RSSR$):

Rule 3: Each $RUCA_i$ in the context **Providing** (C_1) of control action CA_i can be transformed automatically into a new software safety requirement as follows:

$RSSR_i$ = <CA> **must Not be Provided** <TC> **when** <Cs= $\bigcup(\mathcal{P}_1 = v_1, \ldots \mathcal{P}_n = v_n)$> occurred.

Rule 4: Each $RUCA_i$ in the context **Not Providing** (C_2) of control action CA_i can be transformed automatically into a new software safety requirement as follows:

$RSSR_i$ = <CA> **must be Provided when** <Cs= $\bigcup(\mathcal{P}_1 = v_1, \ldots \mathcal{P}_n = v_n)$> occurred.

Algorithm 5.1 shows the process of generating context tables based on the process model variable values and transforming them into formal specification in LTL.

5.3. Automatically Formalise the Safety Requirements

Based on the definition 4.3 and by using rules 3 and 4, each refined software safety requirement $RSSR_i$, which is identified from the refined unsafe control action $RUCA_i$, can be automatically transformed into a formal specification in LTL.

Rule 3 defines three types of software safety requirements, which means that the control action CA_i must not be provided in the type of context TC = **any time , too early or too late** when the critical combination Cs_i of the relevant process model variable values occurred. Each type of software safety can be transformed automatically into formal specification by the following rules:

Rule 3.1: Each $RSSR_i$ derived from the context of providing control action CA_i **any time** (without delay) can be automatically transformed into LTL as:

LTL_i = G ($Cs_i \rightarrow !\ (controlAction == CA_i)$), where $Cs_i = \bigcup(\mathcal{P}_1 = v_1 \wedge \ldots \mathcal{P}_n = v_n)$.

Rule 3.1 means that it always (G) the software controller should not (!) provide a control action CA_i when the values of the critical combination Cs_i have been occurred.

Rule 3.2: Each $RSSR_i$ derived from the context of providing control action CA_i **too early** can be automatically transformed into LTL as:

LTL_i = G (((*controlAction* == CA_i) $\rightarrow$ Cs_i) & (! (*controlAction* == CA_i) U Cs_i)).

Rule 3.2 means that a software controller should always (G) not provide control action CA_i before the occurrence of critical combinations set Cs_i still not become true in the execution path and that it well provides the CA_i when the combination of Cs_i holds.

Rule 3.3: Each $RSSR_i$ derived from the context of providing control action CA_i **too late** can be automatically transformed into LTL as:

LTL_i= G((Cs_i $\rightarrow$ (*controlAction* == CA_i)) & (! $Cs_i U$(*controlAction* == CA_i))).

Rule 3.3 means that the software controller should always (G) not provide a control action CA_i too late while the occurrences of the critical set of combinations has become previously true in the execution path.

Rule 4.1 defines one type of the software safety requirements which is the context of not providing a control action CA_i when it is required. This type can be expressed into LTL by the following rule:

Rule 4.1: Each $RSSR_i$ derived from the context of **Not providing** of control action CA_i can be automatically transformed into LTL as:

LTL_i = G (Cs_i $\rightarrow X$(*controlAction* == CA_i)), where $Cs_i = \bigcup(\mathcal{P}_1 = v_1 \wedge \ldots \mathcal{P}_n = v_n)$.

This rule means that the occurrence of a critical set of combination values always implies that the software controller must provide the control action CA_i at the next time step (X) without any delay.

5.4. Safety-Based Test Case Generation

To generate the safety-based test cases, the information derived from the STPA safety analysis must be integrated into a suitable model which should visualize the process model variables of each software controller and their relations in a control structure diagram. We use the Simulink Stateflow editor to visualize the safe behavioral model by using the Simulink Stateflow diagram notations, which supports the export of the statechart notations as XML specifications. Figure 2.7 shows the XML specifications of the Simulink's Stateflow model.

We use the XML specification of the Simulink Stateflow as an input to the safety-based testing process to check the correctness of the *Safe Test Model* against the STPA-generated safety requirements and generate the safety-based testing cases from the safe test model as follows:

5.4.1. Automatically Transforming a Safe Software Behavioral Model into an SMV Model

To check the correctness of the safe behavioral model and ensure that the safe behavioral model of the software controller satisfies all STPA software safety requirements, the safe behavioral model must be verified against the generated LTL formulae. For this purpose, we developed an algorithm that automatically transforms the SBM model created in the Simulink editor into an input language of a model checker such as SMV (Symbolic Model Verifier), automatically parses the LTL formulae from the STPA data model and includes them into an SMV model. To verify the SMV model against the STPA software safety requirements, we use the NuSMV model checker. In case that the SMV model does not satisfy a given LTL of a software safety requirement, the NuSMV model checker will return a counterexample. A counterexample contains information that shows why the given LTL formula of a software safety requirement is not satisfied. Based on the counterexample's information, the safe behavioral should be modified. As the

```xml
<?xml version="1.0" encoding="utf-8"?>
<ModelInformation Version="1.0">
<Model Name="Thesis">
<P Name="Version">8.7</P>
<P Name="MdlSubVersion">1</P>
<P Name="SavedCharacterEncoding">US-ASCII</P>
</Model>
<Stateflow>
<machine id="17">
<P Name="created">11-Nov-2015 14:11:22</P>
<Children>
<chart id="18">
<P Name="name">Chart</P>
<P Name="decomposition">CLUSTER_CHART</P>
<Children>
<state SSID="3">
<P Name="labelString">State2 entry: var1 = -1;</P>
<P Name="type">OR_STATE</P>
<Children>
<state SSID="12">
<P Name="labelString">subState 3</P>
<P Name="type">OR_STATE</P>
</state>
<state SSID="14">
<P Name="labelString">subState4</P>
<P Name="type">OR_STATE</P>
</state>
<transition SSID="13">
<P Name="labelString"></P>
<src>
</src>
<dst>
<P Name="SSID">12</P>
</dst>
</transition>
<transition SSID="15">
<P Name="labelString">[t2==1]</P>
<src>
<P Name="SSID">12</P>
...

</Children>
</chart>
</Children>
</machine>
</Stateflow>
</ModelInformation>
```

Figure 5.3.: The XML specifications of Simulink's Stateflow model

LTL formula contains information about the state of software controller s_i and the control action *CA*, therefore, the modification of the safe behavioral model involves changes to the transition conditions or the initial values of the variables of the state s_i in which the model violated the given LTL formula. This step continues until the safe behavioral model satisfies all STPA-generated software safety requirements.

The algorithm of generating the SMV model is divided into three sub-algorithms: 1) *generate STPA data model* which parses XML specifications of the STPA project created in XSTAMPP (shown in algorithm 5.2); 2) *generate Stateflow (safe behavioral model) data model* which parses XML specifications of a Stateflow model and generate a tree of Stateflow states (TSf) in which a node represents one Stateflow state (shown in algorithm 5.3); and 3) *generate SMV model* which transforms the STPA data model and Stateflow data model into SMV specifications (shown in algorithm 5.5).

5.4.1.1. **Parsing the STPA project created by XSTAMPP**

Algorithm 5.2 shows the process of parsing the STPA project created by XSTAMPP. The algorithm process accepts the STPA project file F as input. Then, it parses the XML specification of the STPA project into the corresponding data model *DataModel* which represent all data in an STPA project (see lines $1-3$). For each software controller in the control structure diagram, a data model DM_{SW} will be created to store the information about the software controller such as its critical control actions, process model and its variables, software safety requirements and the generated LTL formulae (see lines $4-5$). The algorithm will fetch the information of each software controller and store them in the corresponding lists (see lines $6-9$) and add these lists into the data model of the software controller (see lines $11-14$). The output of this algorithm is a list of the data model of the software controllers in the safety control structure diagram (see line 16).

5.4.1.2. **Parsing the Stateflow model created by Simulink/Matlab**

Algorithm 5.3 shows how to parse the XML specifications of the Stateflow model stored in a Simulink/Matlab file. The input of this algorithm is an XML file

Algorithms 5.2 Generate STPA Data Model

Input: F : A STPA project file
Data:
CAs= a list of control actions,
$PMVs$= a list of process model variables,
$SSRs$ = a list of software safety requirements, and
$LTLs$ = a list of generated LTL formulae of SSR.
$DataModel$= a data model which stores all information of STPA project F.
Output: $DataModel_{SW}$= a list of the data model of the software controller $CO \in F$. **Description:**

URL schemaFile ("*/hazschema.xsd*")
XSModel LoadXMLSchema ($schemaFile$)
DataModel ParseXMLSchema (F)
for each SW_i Controller in $DataModel$ **do**
  Create a new data model DM_{SW} for SW_i Controller.
  Fetch: $CAs \leftarrow DataModel.fetchControlActions()$
  Fetch: $PMV \leftarrow DataModel.fetchProcessModelVariables()$
  Fetch: $SSRs \leftarrow DataModel.fetchSoftwareSafetyRequirements()$
  Fetch: $LTLs \leftarrow DataModel.fetchLTLs()$
  Add $DM_{SW}.CAs \leftarrow CAs$
  Add $DM_{SW}.PMVs \leftarrow PMVs$
  Add $DM_{SW}.SSRs \leftarrow SSRs$
  Add $DM_{SW}.LTLs \leftarrow LTLs$
  Add $DataModel_{SW}[i] \leftarrow DM_{SW}$.
end for
Return $DataModel_{SW}$

of the Simulink Stateflow file (Sf) which contains XML specifications of the Stateflow model. To parse the Stateflow file which we created in the Simulink editor, we first generate XML specifications of the Simulink Stateflow from the Simulink/Matlab editor.

The structure of the Stateflow model allows a multilevel hierarchy of states in which a state $S_{i.j}$ can contain sub-states with different types, where i indicates the number of the level hierarchy of the Stateflow model ($i = 0...n$), j is the number of states, and n is the total number of levels in the Stateflow model. Therefore, the algorithm 5.3 traverses recursively the Stateflow data model based on the depth-first search algorithm to consider all sub-states of the superstate

Algorithms 5.3 Generate a Tree of Stateflow Data

Input: Sf : A Simulink Stateflow file
Data: DM_{Sf} = A data model to store all data of Stateflow in Sf,
S= A list of states of Stateflow Sf.
Output: T_{Sf} = a tree which represents all information of Stateflow states $\in sf$.
Description:

URL schemaFile ("/$Stateflowschema.xsd$")
XSModel LoadXMLSchema ($schemaFile$)
DM_{Sf} ParseXMLSchema (Sf)
Extract all states at level 0: $S \leftarrow DM_{Sf}$.Stateflow.getStates()
Create a state root node $\leftarrow root$
Set ParentID $root \leftarrow$ ParentID $\notin DM_{Sf}.States.IDs$
Name $root \leftarrow$ 'root'
for each State s **in** S **do**
    Create a state child node $\leftarrow node$
    Set ParentID $node.parentID \leftarrow root.ID$.
    Set Data $node.name \leftarrow s.name$
    $node.Id \leftarrow s.SSID$
    $node.setDecomposition \leftarrow s.getDecomposition()$
    $node.setStatesActions \leftarrow s.getStatesActions()$//Entry, During and Exit
    if $s.hasChildren()$==true **then**
        $node.isHasChildren(true)$
        traverseChildren ($node$, s)
    end if
    Add $root.addChild$ ($node$)
end for
    // Extract all transitions between the states.
    T_{Sf}.**setTransitions(**$DM_{Sf}.getTransitions()$**)**
    // Extract all variables of Stateflow.
    T_{Sf}.**setVariables(**$DM_{Sf}.getVariables()$**)**
T_{Sf}.root = $root$
Return T_{Sf}

and add them to the tree of Stateflow. Each Stateflow model has two kinds of state decomposition: OR states (exclusive) and AND states (parallel) [Mat16]. The Stateflow semantics allow every state to have a state decomposition that indicates what type of sub-states the superstate can contain. All sub-states of a superstate $S_{i,j}$ should have the same type of decomposition of the parent state.

5.4.1.3. Generating the tree of the Stateflow model

The algorithm for generating the tree of the Stateflow (shown in algorithms 5.3 & 5.4) starts by parsing the XML specifications of the Simulink's Stateflow *Sf* into the data model DM_{Sf} (see lines $1-3$). A tree Stateflow will be created to store a root node, a list of transitions and the list of the Stateflow variables. As a Stateflow model has no root state, a default node called $root$ will be created to store all information about the superstates at level 0 and assigned its *ParentID* randomly as an integer number that is not assigned to any state in the Stateflow model (see lines $4-7$). Each node stores the following data: id, *name*, *parentID*, T a list of transitions, a list of children (sub-states), the order of execution, a list of the state actions (entry, during and exit actions) and type of decomposition state (*OR State* or *AND State*). All superstates at level 0 in the Stateflow model are added as the children of the default *root* node. For each state $S_{i,j}$, a node will be created to store all information of the state $S_{i,j}$ (see lines $8-14$). If the state $S_{i,j}$ has children, then all its sub-states will be traversed recursively until no more children exist for the superstate (see line 15). Then, a state $node$ will be added as a child of the root node (see line 17). The transitions at this level will be added to a transition list of the Stateflow tree T_{sf} to be used in the next algorithms (see line $21-23$): the *SMVGenerator* algorithm, Extended Finite State Machine model (*EFSMGenerator*) and a truth-table of the EFSM model generator.

5.4.1.4. Generating the SMV model from the STPA and Stateflow data models

Figure 2.5 shows the basic structure of the SMV model as described in [Cav+10]. Each SMV module represents a superstate in the Stateflow model which can contain the following sections: 1) The name of the model with the optional state variable parameters, 2) The declaration of the state variable and their possible values, 3) The initial values of variables and the $states$ variable, 4) The sub-modules of the super module declaration, 5) The transitions of the module, and a list of the LTL formulae. To represent the states of the Stateflow model ($\simeq$ internal state variables of each controller in STPA) in an SMV model, we declare an enumeration variable called *"states"* which contains the names of sub-states of the superstate in the Stateflow model.

Algorithms 5.4 traverseChildren(root, s)

Input: *root* : a root node in the tree T_{Sf}, s: a state in a satateflow data model DM_{Sf}

Description:

```
if s.hasChildren()==ture then
    for each State child in s.getChildren() do
        Create a new node node
        Set node.setName ← child.getName
        nodel.setId ← child.getID
        node.setParentID ← child.getParentID
        node.setDecomposition ← child.getDecomposition()
        node.StatesActions ← child.StatesActions()//Entry, During, Exit
        if child.hasChildren()== ture then
            node.setHasChildren(true)
        end if
          Add root.addChild(node)
          traverseChildren(node, child)
    end for
end if
```

Based on the principles of the SMV model [Cav+10] and Stateflow diagram [Mat16], we develop an algorithm to transform the Stateflow (safe behavioral model) and STPA data objects into an SMV model. Algorithm 5.5–5.6 shows the process of automatically transforming the safe behavioral model and the STPA data models into an input language of the SMV model checker. The algorithm traverses the states of the safe behavioral model recursively and generates the SMV model by parsing the hierarchical levels of the safe behavioral model. The inputs of the algorithm are a tree of Stateflow model T_{Sf} which is created based on algorithms 5.3– 5.4 and the STPA data model $DataModel_{SW}$ of the software controller CO_i, which is generated based on algorithm 5.2 and a node n in the tree T_{Sf}.

The algorithm 4–5 process starts by creating an object of the SMV model which represents all structure data of the SMV model (see line 1). The algorithm takes the root node of the safe behavioral model tree as the input at the first time to create the main module of the SMV model, then it cerate the main module section (see lines $2-6$) and declares the *VAR* section (see line 7). In this section, the algorithm will declare the local variables of the root node and maps their data types to the SMV data types (see lines $8-9$). The algorithm will check whether the variables are declared exactly in the process model of the software controller in the STPA control structure diagram to reduce the time and effort of matching these variables during the verification step (see line 10). If a name of variable or state in the STPA data model does not match any name in the data model of the safe behavioral model, then the algorithm will show a message to the user and return *null* (see line 49).

The SMV model does not support the same basic data types (int, double, single) as the data types which are declared in the Stateflow model, it supports only a finite range type as integer range $min...max$ value. Therefore, the algorithm should map the data types (int, double or single) into a finite range which starts with a minimum value and ends with a maximum value of integer data type. The enumeration data types are declared into the Stateflow model as a class which is saved in a separate file and not in the XML specifications of Stateflow model. Therefore, the algorithm checks each variable with enumeration data type whether it is a process model variable in the STPA data model or not. In case the enumeration variable is a process model variable, the algorithm takes its values as they are defined in the STPA process model variable values. Otherwise, the algorithm creates an empty bracket {} for the values of the enumeration variable and prompts the user to determine the values of this variable (see lines $11-15$).

Next, the algorithm checks whether the root state $root$ has children states and which of them has children too (see line $16-20$). In case that a child $node$ of $root$ has children, then the algorithm declares a sub-module for this child $node$. Then, the algorithm takes all variables of the current state $node$ to create a list of the parameters of the sub- module (see line 18). Next, the algorithm parses the sub-states of the superstate and creates the variable *"states"* with a list of the names of the sub-states as values (see lines $21-24$).

The algorithm will create the section *"Assign"* to initial the states and variables of the SMV model (see line 25). The algorithm will create the *initial* expression of the *"states"* variable. Each data variable will also be initialised with the minimum value of its data type such as a variable with a numeric data type with zero,

Algorithms 5.5 generateSMV(T_{Sf}, $DataModel_{SW}$, n)

Input: T_{Sf} : a tree data model of safe behavioral model, $DataModel_{SW}$: a STPA data model of controller CO_i, n: is a node in tree T_{Sf}.
Output: SMV_i: an SMV object represents the data of SMV model.
Description:

Create a $SMV_i \leftarrow$ SMV model object
if (n.isRoot ()==true) **then**
    Set header of $SMV_i \leftarrow$ **'Module main'**
else
    $SMV_i \leftarrow$ **'Module'** root.getName() (root.getVariables)
end if
Set VAR section of $SMV_i \leftarrow$ **'VAR'**
Parse Variables $SMV_i.setVariables() \leftarrow T_{Sf}.getVariables()$
Map data type of SMV variables into SMV data types.
if (ValidateSTPADataModel ($n.getVaraibles()$, $DataModel_{Sw}$) **then**
    if ($v.getType()! =$ "$Enum$") **then**
        Declare each variable as $v.getName()$: v.getType();
    else
        $v.getName()$: {}; // an empty bracket
    end if
    if (n.isSubModule==true) **then**
        for each s ∈ n.getChildren() **do**
            Declare $Sub\_$+s.getName($n.getVariables()$)($n.getVariableNames()$)
        end for
    end if
    Declare $states$ variable in $SMV \leftarrow$ **'states'**
    for each s ∈ n.getChildren() **do**
        states $\leftarrow s.getName()$
    end for
    Set ASSIGN section of $SMV \leftarrow$ **'ASSIGN'**
    initial each v of $SMV_i \leftarrow$
    init(v.getName()) :=initial_Value;
    Parse Transitions $T \leftarrow n$.getTransitions()
    Set Next section of T of n state
    SMV_i.← **'next'** (states) := case
    for each t ∈ T **do**
        $states := t.Source\&t.Condition : t.Destination$;
        TRUE: states ; esac
    end for

Algorithms 5.6 generateSMV (T_{Sf}, *DataModel*$_{SW}$, n) (continued)

35: **if** (n.isRoot ()==true) **then**
36: **for each** v $\in$ n.getVariables () **do**
37: SMV_i.← **'next'** (v.getName()) := case
38: states=n.getSource(): n.getEntryDuringExit(v.getFunction())
39: TRUE: v.getName (); esac;
40: **end for**
41: **end if**
42: SMV_i ← **'esac;'**
43: **if** (n.hasChildren()) **then**
44: **for** s $\in$ $root$.getChildren() **do**
45: SMV_i ← generateSMV(T_{Sf}, DCs_i, s)
46: **end for**
47: **end if**
48: **else**
49: **Show** "STPA variables do not match Sf variables" & **Set** SMV_i ← null
50: **end if**
51: SMV_i← LTLSPEC "DCs_i.getLTL()
52: **Return** SMV_i.

Boolean with FALSE and enumeration variable with the first value (see in lines $26-27$). Next, the algorithm will parse all transitions of the current state $node$ and create the *next* expressions for the *"states"* variable (see lines 28–34). The *next* expressions of $states$ variable refer to the transition relations of current state $node$ with other states in the model (the truth-table). The *next* expressions of the $states$ variable are expressed as follows:

```
 next(states):= case
states=<sub-state> : <nextstate>
...
1: {All sub-states}; esac;
```

To create the *next* expressions for each data variable, the algorithm parses the *Entry, During and Exit* actions of the current state and extracts all actions of each variable (see lines $35-41$). The *next* expressions of the data variables refer to the values of variables in the next state. The *next* expressions of each data variable are expressed as follows:

```
next(variable):= case
states = <state> & transition: <nextValue>
....
```

The algorithm will continue parsing the superstate in the tree of the safe behavioral model (Stateflow) till all superstates have been visited (see lines 43–48). The generated SMV specifications of each sub-module and the main module will be saved as a string into a stack object. Finally, the algorithm will fetch the LTL formulae from the STPA data model object and add them at the end of the main-module section (see lines 50–51).

To check the correctness of the generated SMV model and the safe behavioral model, we run the NuSMV model checker to verify whether the SMV model contains errors and verify it against the STPA software safety requirements expressed in the LTL formulae and saved to the SMV model.

5.4.2. Automatically generating the Safe Test Model from the Safe Software Behavioral Model

After ensuring the correctness of the generated SMV model of the safe behavioral model (Stateflow model), the safe behavioral model which uses the notations of the Simulink's Stateflow should be transformed into the EFSM notation. For this purpose, we develop an algorithm to map the Stateflow tree of the safe behavioral model and its truth-table into an EFSM model. The algorithm 5.7–5.8 shows the process of transforming the tree of the Stateflow model into an EFSM model. The idea here is to eliminate the hierarchical and concurrent structure of the Stateflow model (flattened and broadcast communication) and transform them into the EFSM notations by considering the state decomposition (exclusive or parallel).

The algorithm 5.7–5.8 starts by taking the root node of the Stateflow tree T_{Sf} as the root node of the EFSM model and the truth-table of the Stateflow as the truth-table of the EFSM model (see line 1). The Stateflow semantic supports multi-hierarchy levels of states, whereas the EFSM model does not. Therefore, the truth-table of the EFSM model must not have any source or destination

Algorithms 5.7 GenerateEFSM (T_{Sf})

Input: T_{Sf} : a tree of Stateflow model,
Output: $EFSM$: a Java object represent all data of EFSM
Description:

```
Create StateNode root ← T_Sf.getRoot()
Get TruthTable truthTable ← T_Sf.getTruthTable()
if root.hasChildren()==ture then
    Set Initial state ← T_Sf.getInitialState( )
    while isHasSuperState(truthTable) do
        for Transition t ∈ truthTable do
            StateNode src ← t.getSourceNode ()
            StateNode dest ← t.getDestinationNode ()
            if src.isSuper() & !(dest.isSuper()) then
                get children ← src.getChildren()
                for child ∈ children do
                    updateTruthTable (child, dest, t, truthTable)
                end for
            else
                if !(src.isSuper()) & dest.isSuper() then
                    if dest.Decomp('AND_STATE') then
                        get children ← dest.getSubSates();
                        for child ∈ children do
                            updateTruthTable (src, child, t, truthTable)
                        end for
                    else
                        if dest.Decomp('OR_STATE') then
                            S_D ← getDefaultState(dest)
                            updateTruthTable (src, S_D, t, truthTable)
                        end if
                    end if
                end if
                if src.isSuper() & dest.isSuper() & dest.Decomp('OR_STATE') then
                    get srcChildren ← src.getSubSates();
                    get def ← dest.getDefaultState();
                    for s ∈ srcchildren do
                        updateTruthTable (s, def, t, truthTable)
                    end for
                end if
```

Algorithms 5.8 GenerateEFSM (T_{Sf}) (continued)

```
35:                 if src.isSuper()& dest.isSuper()&dest.Decomp('AND_STATE')
   then
36:                     get srcChildren ← src.getSubSates();
37:                     get destChildren ← dest.getSubSates();
38:                     for s ∈ srcchildren do
39:                         for d ∈ destchildren do
40:                             updateTruthTable (s, d, t, truthTable)
41:                         end for
42:                     end for
43:                 else
44:                     if !(src.isSuper())& !(dest.isSuper()) then
45:                         updateTruthTable (src, dest, t, truthTable)
46:                     end if
47:                 end if
48:             end if
49:         end for
50:     end while
51: end if
52: Add EFSM.setTruthTable ← truthTable
53: Add EFSM.setStates ← T_Sf.getStates()
54: Return EFSM.
```

node as a superstate (a state that has children). The idea here is to investigate the truth-table of Stateflow and update the destination and source parent state with its sub-states. At the beginning, the algorithm checks whether there is a superstate in the truth-table (see lines $2-3$). For each transition $t \in T$ in the truth-table, the algorithm will identify its source and destination states and create two state nodes (see lines 6–8). Next, the algorithm will check their state decomposition as follows:

- If source state $src \in T_{sf}$ of transition t is a **superstate** with a state decomposition "OR_STATE" or "AND_STATE" and the destination node $dest \in T_{sf}$ is **not superstate**. Each sub-state of src state must be linked to the destination state $dest$ by creating a new transition with the same information of transition $T \in T_{sf}.TruthTable$ for each sub-state and only update the source with sub-state (see lines $9-13$).

- If source state $src \in T_{sf}$ is **not superstate** and the destination state $dest \in T_{sf}$ is **superstate** with a state decomposition "AND_STATE". All sub-states of $dest$ state should be identified and linked with the source state (see line $15-20$). Algorithm 5.9will create a new transition for each sub-state of $dest$, where source is src and destination is the sub-state of destination.
- If source state $src \in T_{sf}$ is **not superstate** and the destination state $dest \in T_{sf}$ is **superstate** with a state decomposition "OR_STATE". The default state $defaultState$ of superstate $dest$ (a default state is a state which has a default transition) should be identified (see lines $22-27$). Algorithm 5.9 will create a new transition and set its source as src and its destination as the default state of destination.
- If source state $src \in T_{sf}$ is **superstate** with a state decomposition "OR_STATE" or "AND_STATE" and the destination state $dest \in T_{sf}$ is **superstate** with a state decomposition "OR_STATE". All sub-states of src state should be identified and linked with a default state of $dest$ state (see lines $28-34$). Algorithm 5.9 will create a new transition for each sub-state of src and its source is src and its destination is the default state of destination $dest$ state.
- If source state $src \in T_{sf}$ is **superstate** with a state decomposition "OR_STATE" or "AND_STATE" and the destination state $dest \in T_{sf}$ is **superstate** with a state decomposition "AND_STATE". All sub-states of src state should be identified and linked with all sub-states of $dest$ state (see lines $35-43$). Algorithm 5.9 will create a new transition for each sub-state of src and its source is src and its destination is the sub-state of destination $dest$ state.
- If source state $src \in T_{sf}$ is **not superstate** and the destination state $dest \in T_{sf}$ is **not superstate**. A transition t will be added into the truth-table (see lines $44-46$).

The algorithm runs continuously till no superstate exist in the truth-table. All sub-states (without children) in the Stateflow model tree will be taken as the states of the EFSM model. Also, all data variables of the Stateflow model and the actions of the state (entry, exist, during) will be added into the states of EFSM.

Algorithms 5.9 UpdateTruthTable (t, src, $dest$, $truthTable$)

Input: t : a transition in the truth-table, src : a source node of transition t, $dest$: a destination node of transition t, $truthTable$: a truthTable of Stateflow tree T_{sf}
Description:

```
1: create new Transition t_new
2: set data t_new ← t
3: update t_new.setSrc(src)
4: update t_new.setDest(dest)
5: add truthTable ← t_new
```

5.4.3. Automatically Generating Safety-Based Test Cases

The final step is to generate the test cases from the safe test model (extended finite state machine) which are constructed from the safe behavioral model.

We developed a random walk-based algorithm for automatic test case generation from the safe test model. We implemented three search-based algorithms (e.g. depth-first search, breadth-first search, and both combined depth-breadth-first search). The idea behind here is to select a state in the safe test model as a start node and transform into a Java Script function at run time. The Java script function takes the variables which are declared in the state actions (Entry, during, Exit) of each as parameters and executes the state actions to update the values of the variables. The return value of the function will be determined based on the data type of each variable which is declared in the Simulink Stateflow model. Next, the algorithm will check the transition conditions of a state to determine which is the next state. During traversing the safe test model, the information of the visited states (path sequences) will be saved in a test suite.

Generating test cases from a model usually leads to an infinite number of possible test cases. Therefore, it is necessary to choose a suitable test coverage criteria to manage the generating process. In our algorithm, we identify three test coverage criteria: 1) *state coverage* which is the number of visited states divided by the total number of the states of the model, 2) *transition coverage* is the number of the executed transitions divided by the total number of the transitions, 3) *STPA safety requirements coverage* in which each STPA software safety requirement should be covered at least in one test case to trace how the

STPA-generated software safety requirements are covered into the generated test cases. To measure the STPA SSR coverage, we define a *safety requirements traceability* matrix between the generated safe test model and STPA software safety requirements to manage the quality of the test case generating process and measure the coverage of STPA software safety requirements in the generated safety-based test cases. As the safe test model of the safe behavioral model is constrained with STPA safety requirements (step 2) and contains the process model variables as states, the algorithm will automatically generate the traceability matrix ($TM = SSR \times TN$, where $SSR \in DCs$ of the STPA data model and TN transition conditions $\in T_{Sf}$).

Algorithm 5.10 shows how to generate the traceability matrix TM by calculating the similarity degree between each STPA-generated software safety requirement(SSR) and the transitions condition (TN) of the safe behavioral model and the input state actions of the source state of transition condition TN. The similarity degree is calculated by the following equation:

$$Sim_{(SSR,TN)} = \frac{|\#\text{Total No. matched tokens between (SSR, TN)}|}{|\#\text{Max No. tokens in (SSR, TN)}\ |} \times 100 \quad (5.1)$$

Algorithm 5.10 takes a STPA-generated software safety requirement (SSR), a transition condition TN, the source state of the transition condition TN and a minimum degree of similarity ($maxSimilarity$) which should be between 5% ... 100% and entered by the user. To compare between the STPA-generated software safety requirements and transition conditions, the algorithm construct at first the full transition information by including the name of source state and the control action which is provided in this state to the transition condition. The algorithm creates the full transition information by adding the source state src and the control action $controlAction$ to the transition condition TN. The full transition condition will be constructed as follows:

Full Transition $\leftarrow$ *{states=src.getName() and contorlAction=src.getAction() and src.getTransitionCondition (TN)}*

The algorithm calculates the similarity degree based on the equation 5.1. If the similarity degree is greater than the minimum degree of similarity, then the algorithm will create an item in the traceability matrix for the software safety requirement SSR and the transition condition TN. The algorithm also allows the

Algorithms 5.10 Generate Traceability Matrix (SSR, TN, src, $minSimilarity$)

Input: SSR: a STPA-generated software safety requirement, TN: a transition condition in a safe test model extracted from SBM. src: a source node of transition condition Tn.
$minSimilarity$: a minimum degree of similarity between 5% ... 100%.
Output TM: a traceability matrix. **Description:**

```
Add TN ← states = src.getName()
Add TN ← controlAction = src.getAction().getName()
tokenize SSR[] ← SSR
tokenize TN[] ← TN
get max_Tokens ← max (SSR[], TN[])
inital Sim ← 0
inital matched_Tokens ← 0
inital i ← 0
while i < max_Tokens do
    inital j ← 0
    while j < max_Tokens − 1 do
        if SSR[i] == TN[j] then
            matched_Tokens = matched_Tokens + 1
        end if
        j = j + 1
    end while
    i = i + 1
end while
Sim_{SSR,TN} =(matched_Tokens / max_Tokens) × 100
if Sim_{SSR,TN} > minSimilarity% then
    Add TM ← SSR × TN
end if
Return TM.
```

user to set the maximum similarity degree between 5..100% before generating the safety-based test cases.

Algorithm 5.11 shows how to generate the test cases from the safe test model. It takes the generated Safe Test Model (*STM*), a Traceability Matrix TM, a list of the test coverage criteria *CC*, a number of test steps which is the total number of executions of the algorithm and a stop condition which is a test coverage criteria to stop the execution of the algorithm when it reaches 100%. The process of generating the test cases from the safe test model can be described as follows:

Algorithms 5.11 Generate Safety-based Test Cases(STM, TM,CC, $TestSteps$, $StopConiditon$)

Input: STM: a safe test model extracted from SBM, TM: a traceability matrix, CC: is a list of the test coverage criteria, $TestSteps$ is the total number of execution algorithms, $StopCondition$: a condition to stop the execution process.
Output TS: a list of test suites, each test suite should contain a list one test case TC.
Description:

```
1: Initial step ← 0
2: while step < TestSteps do
3:     Choose start state ← STM.getRandomState()
4:     Choose end state ← STM.getRandomState()
5:     Create a new test suite ts
6:     if StopConiditon < 100.0% then
7:         Randomly Generate_Tes_InputData ()
8:         Walk TC_i ← GenerateTestCasesByDFS (start, end)
9:         Add ts ← TC_i
10:        Walk TC_j ← GenerateTestCasesByBFS (start)
11:        Add ts ← TC_j
12:    else
13:        if StopConiditon==100.0% then
14:            Calculate_Coverage_Criteria()
15:            STOP
16:        end if
17:    end if
18:    ADD TS ← ts
19:    Calculate_Coverage_Criteria()
20:    unvisitedTransitions(STM)
21:    unvisitedStates(STM)
22:    Initial step ← step + 1
23: end while
24: Return TS.
```

1. The algorithm starts by selecting a random state as the start state and a state as the end state from the safe test model to generate all possible paths between them (see lines 3 – 4).

2. A new test suite ts will be created to store all the generated test cases.
3. Generate for each input data variable a random value between its minimum and maximum values which are identified by the user (see line 7).
4. Walk randomly by using the depth-first algorithm, all possible paths between the start and end states will be identified. The path here means a sequence of the visited states and their transitions. We also use the breadth-first algorithm combined with depth-first algorithm to identify all possible paths PT from start state to achieve a good test coverage criteria (see line $8-11$).
    - For each transition t in path $pt \in PT$, its transition condition will be transformed into a Java Script function. The test input variables in will be passed as an input of a Java Script function. To execute this function at the run time, we use the Java Script Engine which invokes the function with values of input data parameters and returns the result.
    - For each state s in path pt, the state actions (Entry, During, Exit) will be eliminated and transformed into Java Script functions. These will be executed to update the values of each local loc or output variable out of each state.
    - Create a new test case tc. Each test case will store the information about the sequence path pt such as: *id* is a number of the test case, *id_Ts* which is the number of the test suite, *id_SSR* which is the number of the software safety requirement, *preconditions and actions* which is the sequence of the local variables of states in the path pt and their updated values, and *postconditions* which is the sequence of output variables and their values.
5. Check whether the test case tc has been covered in any test suite. If it hasn't, tc will be added to the test suite ts (see line 13).
6. Calculate the test coverage criteria and check the stop condition of the algorithm (see line 14).

7. Change status of all states and transitions in the safe test model to unvisited to generate a new sequence path (see line $20-21$).
8. The algorithm will be continued (repeat 1-8) till the stop condition is achieved (100%) or the number of executions the algorithm has been reached to the total number of the test steps.

Ultimately, the time spent during test case generation process, the values of the test coverage criteria and a list of test suits and their test cases with the related software safety requirements will be automatically saved into a CSV file.

5.5. Summary

In this chapter, we presented the automation support for the STPA SwISs approach. We showed how to transform the informal textual safety requirements into formal specification in LTL to enable the verification activities of the system against the STPA-generated safety requirements. We also discussed how to model the STPA results into a suitable software behavior model for safety-based test generation. We explored how to automatically generate the SMV verification model from the safe behavioral model. Finally, we explained the algorithms of the safety-based test case generation process from the safe behavioral model.

The automation support algorithms are implemented in our tool support to reduce the effort required to manually generate the context tables, refine the unsafe control actions, generate unsafe scenarios and perform safety verification activities with the model checker and the testing approach.

Chapter 6

Tool Support

> *I think, fundamentally, open source does tend to be more stable software. It's the right way to do things.*
>
> — *Linus Torvalds*

In this chapter, we describe the tool support that we developed to support the application of the safety engineering approach based on STPA for software-intensive systems as well as the STAMP methodologies STPA and CAST.

6.1. XSTAMPP

The increase in the usage of STAMP methodologies has fostered the need for developing a support tool to assist safety engineers in performing the safety analysis as well as the accident analysis. For this purpose, we developed tool called XSTAMPP[1] (eXtensible STAMP Platform) [AW15b]. XSTAMPP is a software tool developed to serve the widespread adoption and use of STAMP methodologies (STPA and CAST) in different domains. It is also developed to support the safety engineering approach based STPA called (STPA SwISs) to automatically generate the context tables which are used to refine the safety requirements and automatically transform the refined safety requirements into a formal specification in Linear Temporal Logic (LTL) to support verification activities. XSTAMPP supports automatically verifying the LTL formulae of the STPA-generated safety requirements with model checkers such as NuSMV and SPIN. Furthermore, XSTAMPP was also extended to automatically generate the safety-based test cases directly from the STPA results and Simulink's Stateflow. XSTAMPP is an open

[1] http://www.xstampp.de/

source, plug-in-based, extensible software platform using the Eclipse Rich Client Platform (RCP)[1] which makes our platform easier to extend and to integrate independent components. XSTAMPP is built to be flexible to be extended by including different user interface editors for the STAMP components and to be used by different users in different application areas. The last version of XSTAMPP 2.0.2, the source code of XSTAMPP and its plug-ins are available at our repository[2].

6.1.1. XSTAMPP Architecture

As shown in figure 6.1, the XSTAMPP platform architecture mainly consists of four components:

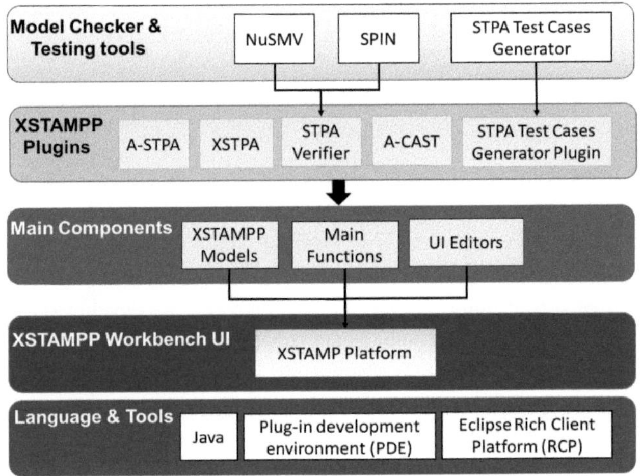

Figure 6.1.: The XSTAMPP Architecture

- **STAMP Components** The main components which are used during the application of the STAMP/STPA approach: 1) STAMP data lists (e.g. Hazards list, accidents list, system goals and design constraints, safety requirements, corresponding safety constraints and control actions), 2) STAMP

[1] http://www.eclipse.org/
[2] http://sourceforge.net/projects/stampp

diagrams (e.g. hierarchical and detailed safety control structures, and process models diagram); and 3) STAMP Tables (e.g. unsafe control actions table and causal factors analysis table).

- **STAMP Components Editors** As an external representation, each STAMP component is represented by an independent Eclipse user interface editor which is tightly integrated into the platform workbench UI. Each editor allows a safety analyst to edit a STAMP component in a separate user interface.
- **Workbench User Interface** The workbench UI contains the infrastructure for views and UI editors. All UI editors of STAMP components, views and perspectives are located in the Workbench UI.
- **XSD Specification Template** As an internal representation, each STAMP component editor is always associated with an XML element that documents the input data from a safety analyst in the user interface editor. All XML elements will be saved to and restored from a saved XSD[1] file with extension *.haz for a whole project.
- **Plug-in Development Environment (PDE)** PDE provides custom extension points which can be extended with new software components. A software component called a plug-in is a component that provides a certain type of service within the context of the Eclipse workbench[2].
- **Eclipse Rich Client Platform (RCP)** RCP provides an inherently extensible application framework that allows the seamless integration of independent software modules into a software application.

6.1.2. Design and implementation

The following is a description of the implementation and design details of the XSTAMPP platform:

From the implementation point of view, we developed the STAMP platform based on the Eclipse RCP platform and XSD specifications to facilitate versioning, backup and possible future integration with other tools. Built upon RCP,

[1] http://www.w3.org/XML/Schema
[2] https://eclipse.org

XSTAMPP provides core functionality that makes it easier to extend in the future. The new architecture of our platform supports to add new plug-ins into the workbench UI. We developed each STAMP component editor as a plug-in which can be easily integrated and extended. For each STPA component, we also provided an XML element template which acts as an internal representation of the STAMP component data. These features make our platform easy to extend in the future and to implement new requirements and extensions for STPA and CAST as well.

From the design point of view, the STAMP platform allows the safety analyst to create and open many projects by a New/open project wizard. The current version of XSTAMPP supports only to create and open STPA projects. However, XSTAMPP has a potential to include the CAST project as well. Each project will be viewed in the project explorer as a tree which contains the basic components of the main steps of STPA (as shown in Figure 6.2). For instance, an STPA project will appear with three sub-trees which are: a sub-tree of the fundamentals of analysis (e.g. system description, accidents, hazards), a sub-tree for the control structure diagram and a sub tree the STPA data tables e.g. unsafe control actions and causal factor tables.

From the functionality point of view, the new platform allows safety analysts to select and add new views to his/her project explorer such as a view of the hierarchical control structure, a view of the control structure diagram at a detailed level and the context table of the process model variables. Unlike A-STPA, the new STAMP platform allows the safety analysts to open different user interface editors in the platform workbench at the same time, order and manage them in one view. That provides a safety analyst with the capability to view many user interface editors of the project in the workbench. Furthermore, the new platform enables the safety analysts to export the results of analysis in different formats such as PDF, JPEG or Excel for a whole project or for each user interface view.

Figure 6.2 shows the main workbench of XSTAMPP which is divided into three main parts: a project explorer, the user interface viewer and the toolbox. The safety engineers can use XSTAMPP to perform CAST accident analysis and STPA safety analysis. They can create and open two different types of XSTAMPP projects: STPA safety analysis and CAST accident analysis in the project explorer.

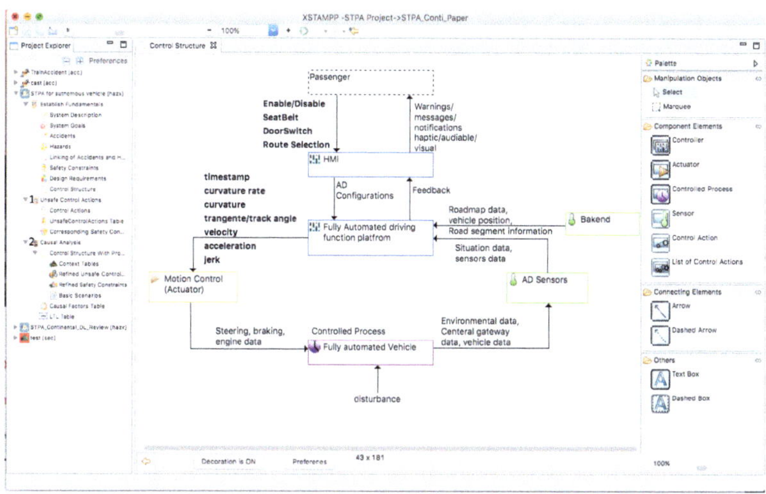

Figure 6.2.: The main workbench UI of XSTAMPP

Any XSTAMPP project includes all necessary components to document the results of applying STPA and CAST in different domains such as fundamentals of analysis, drawing the control structure diagram of the system, editing STAMP data (i.e. the unsafe control actions, causal factors, safety roles and responsibilities).

6.1.3. XSTAMPP Plug-ins

XSTAMPP includes different Eclipse plug-ins as follows:

6.1.3.1. A-STPA

A-STPA[1] (Automated STPA) [AW14a] is an open source tool to help transform STPA (System-Theoretic Process Analysis) to an executable STPA which automates the activities of STPA. We develop the A-STPA tool to assist safety analysts in performing STPA. Moreover, it will give the safety analysts different views on the STPA hazard analysis process. We discuss the design of the tool and illustrate

[1]http://www.xstampp.de/a-stpa.html

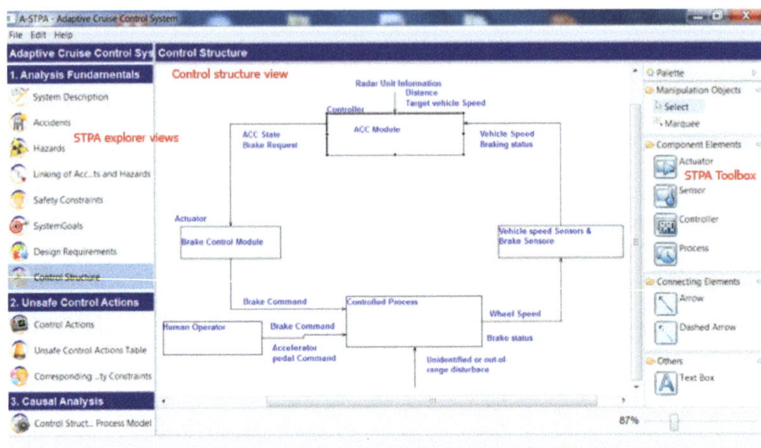

Figure 6.3.: The main workbench UI of A-STPA standalone version

its usage. So far, it is still an early version but it can already help the safety analysts in avoiding consistency defects. We are confident that A-STPA will become a powerful tool support for STPA. A-STPA is developed as a standalone version based on the Eclipse platform. Figure 6.3 shows the main workbench UI of A-STPA. A-STPA has the following main functions:

1. Edit the fundamentals of the analysis
2. Link the conducted information during step 1 to the other components in the next steps such as the hazards link to the accidents and safety constraints which are derived from the hazards.
3. Draw the control structure diagram
4. Edit tables such as the control actions table, unsafe control action table and causal factors table
5. Augment the control structure diagram with a process model
6. Export and import the STPA hazard analysis results

However, the stand-alone version has a some of shortcoming in terms of extensibility, functionality, designing and editing issues. Based on the A-STPA stand-alone version, we developed A-STPA as an Eclipse plug-ins based to support the application of STPA in XSTAMPP. In A-STPA plug-in version, we enhanced the usability and functionality of A-STPA by removing the shortcomings of A-STPA. We built a new editor for documenting a large number of unsafe control actions and causal factors. Moreover, we improved the drawing features of the control structure diagram by implementing a new component as a dashed box component to add comments or to group some components in one box and a component of the control actions list in which the safety analyst can draw and link multi-control actions to one arrow.

6.1.3.2. XSTPA

XSTPA[1] (Automated tool support for the extended approach to STPA) [AW16] is an Eclipse plug-in to automate the extended approach to STPA proposed by Thomas and our improvements [AW15a] to automatically generate the context table and unsafe software scenarios. XSTPA uses a combinatorial testing algorithm [KKL13] to automatically generate the context table and identify a minimal combination of process model variables for large and complex systems. XSTPA uses a Java library for the combinatorial testing algorithm called ACTS[2] which was developed by the American National Institute of Standards and Technology to generate combination sets of t parameters with n values (context tables). Furthermore, XSTPA automatically generates the hazardous rules and allows the safety analyst to refine the unsafe control actions and it automatically refines the safety requirements and transforms them into formal specifications in LTL.

From the functionality view, when the safety analyst augments the process model into a controller component in the control structure diagram view, the XSTPA editor (as shown in Fig 6.4) will automatically appear under the control structure diagram UI view with necessary information about the controllers, their process model variables with their values and the control actions on the control structure diagram. The safety analyst has to choose which control action

[1] `http://www.xstampp.de/xstpa.html`
[2] `http://csrc.nist.gov/groups/SNS/acts/index.html`

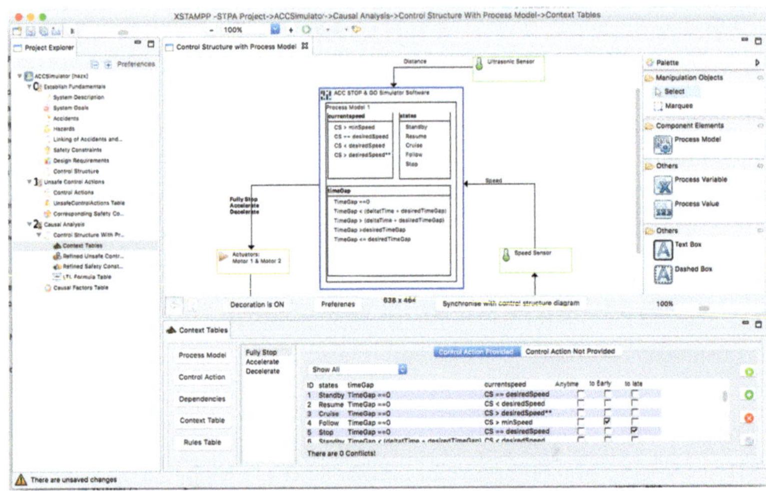

Figure 6.4.: The XSTPA plug-in in the XSTAMPP workbench UI

is safety-critical to generate its context tables. Then, the safety analyst has to determine the dependencies D between the control action and its relevant process model variables in two contexts (C_1= providing and C_2 =not providing). For each dependency relation, XSTPA will automatically generate an input file N as input to the ACTS algorithm to automatically generate the context tables of each safety-critical control action. The input file of ACTS is a text file with the following format [KKL13]:

```
[System]
Name:  Adaptive Cruise Control System (ACC)
[Parameter]
ACC_Mode (enum): Standby, Cruise, Follow
Brake (enum) : NotApplied,  Applied
Distance (enum): D>= safeDistance, D<safeDistance
[Relation]
[Constraint]
ACC_Mode !='Off'
```

The [**System**] section contains the information about the STPA project and the [**Parameter**] section contains the definition of process model variables and their values. All process model variables are defined as *enum* data type to accept different kinds of values of the process model variables. The [**Relation**] section is an optional section which defines the strengths between the process model variables. For example, the ACC system has 3 process model variables, then the first relation can be created that consists of all the process model variables with strength 1 or 2. The safety analyst can define a custom relation when some process model variables have a higher degree of interaction or they are closely related to each other. The [**Constraint**] section is an optional section which includes the Boolean conditions that combinations must satisfy to be valid. For instance, the constraint (ACC_Mode ! ='Off') will exclude all rows in the generated context table of process model variable *ACC_Mode* which contain the value *off*.

When the safety analyst clicks on the generate button in the context table, XSTPA will automatically generate the combinations of the process model variables $CS_i = \bigcup(\mathcal{P}_{i,1} \wedge \ldots \mathcal{P}_{i,n})$. From setting UI view, the safety analyst can apply different combination coverage on the generated results such as pairwise coverage or t-way coverage to minimize the number of the combination sets. Pairwise coverage means that for each 2 process model variables, every possible combination of values of these 2 variables must be covered in at least one combination. T-way coverage means that for t process model variables, every possible combination of values of these t variables must be covered in at least one combination [KKL13].

XSTPA can automatically show the conflicted combination sets. The conflicted combination sets mean that two or more combination sets have the same values of the process model variables in the both two contexts (providing and not providing) of one control action. If the safety analyst selects any combination as hazardous in any context, XSTPA will automatically express them as Boolean expressions with an AND operator. Finally, the XSTPA will generate automatically the LTL formulae of the hazardous combination sets of a safety critical system. The results of XSTPA can also be exported as PDFs, images and CVS sheets.

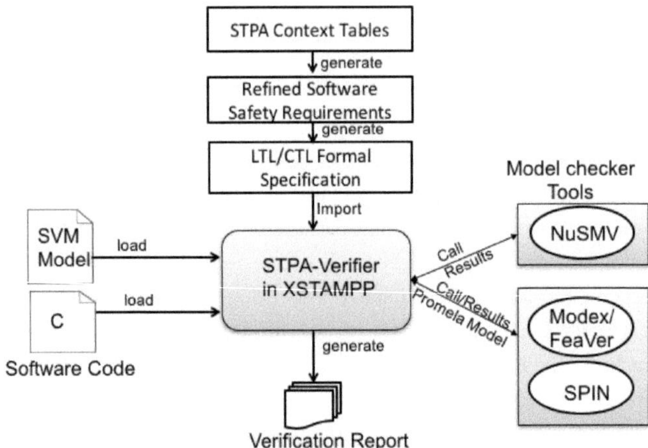

Figure 6.5.: The STPA Verifier process

6.1.3.3. STPA Verifier

STPA Verifier[1] [AW16] is an Eclipse plug-in developed to verify the STPA safety requirements with model checking tools such as SPIN and NuSMV. The STPA-generated safety requirements are automatically transformed into formal specification in LTL (linear Temporal Logic).

As shown in figure 6.5, the STPA verifier plug-in fetches all LTL formulae from XSTPA and allows user to load the verification model of the system (Promela or SMV Model). Furthermore, STPA verifier provides a configuration view of each model checker (SPIN and NuSMV) to enable user to configure the model checker with the necessary parameters. It also allows users to extract the Promela model from C Code of the software by using the Modex tool. The STPA Verifier shows the results of each LTL formula in the table with different values such as a syntax error, success, failed (counterexample) and incomplete. It also shows the verification results for each LTL formula with information of how many states the model checker visited to validate the LTL formula, how many transitions, memory space which is spent during search, time which the model checker spent.

[1] `http://www.xstampp.de/stpaverifier.html`

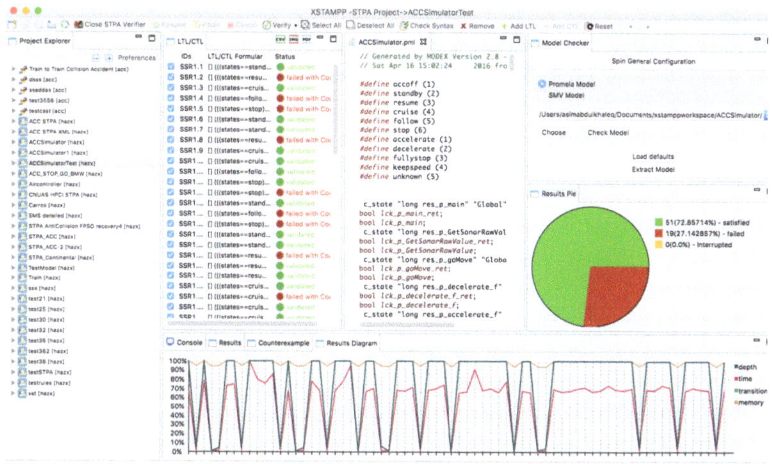

Figure 6.6.: The main views of STPA Verifier in XSTAMPP

Figure 6.6 shows the main views of the STPA verifier in XSTAMPP.

6.1.3.4. STPA TCGenerator

STPA TCGenerator[1] is a stand-alone tool written in Java based on the NetBeans platform. STPA TCGenerator is developed to generate the safety-based test cases directly from STPA safety analysis results. STPA TCGenereator parses the STPA file project created in XSTAMPP and the safe behavioral model which is created with Simulink's Stateflow editor to automatically generate the SMV model and check the correctness of the safe behavioral model, eliminate the safe test model and generate safety-based test cases (shown in Figure 6.7).

We summarise the main functions of the STPA TCGenerator as follows:

- Parse the STPA data model which is documented in XML specification into Java objects.
- Parse the XML specification of the Simulink Stateflow model into Java objects.

[1] `http://www.xstampp.de/STPATCGenerator.html`

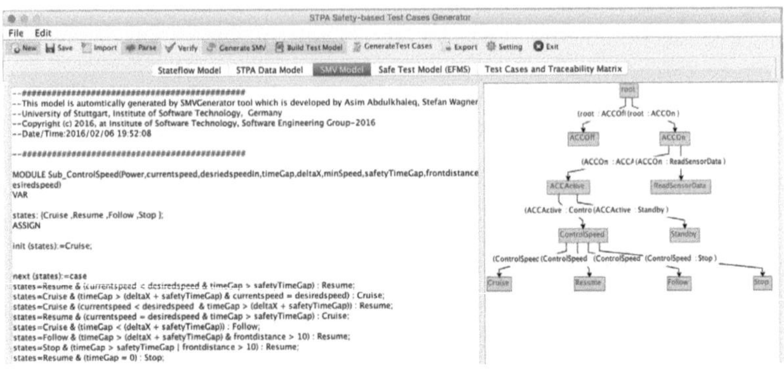

Figure 6.7.: The main views of STPA TCGenerator(Standalone version)

- Based on the STPA data model and the Simulink Stateflow model, the tool automatically generates the SMV model.
- Check the consistency between the STPA data model and the specification of Simulink Stateflow and provides the results to the user (e.g. matched, does not match, and unknown).
- Verify the generated SMV model against the generated LTL of the STPA safety requirements.
- From the Simulink Stateflow model which is verified against the STPA safety requirements, the tool automatically transforms the Simulink Stateflow model into the extended finite state model for testing purposes.
- Generate the tractability matrix between STPA safety requirements and the Simulink Stateflow specifications.
- Allow the user to add the test input data for each input variable.
- Allow the user to configure the test case generation process by adding a number of test steps and selecting the test case generation algorithm and the test coverage.

The STPA TCGenerator tool accepts two files as input: an STPA project with extension haz. or .hazx and a Stateflow model as XML file. The STPA TCGenerator

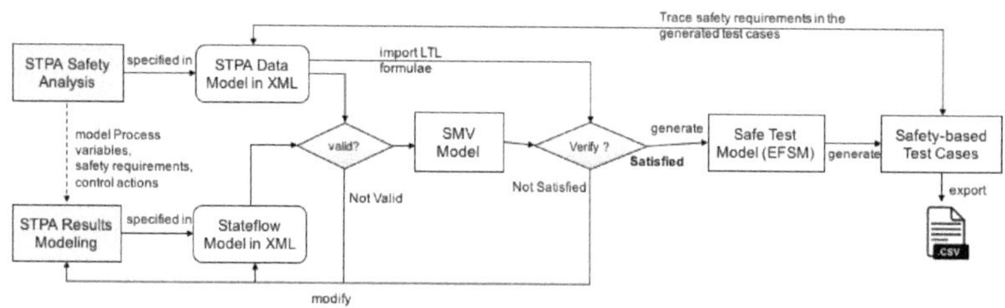

Figure 6.8.: The process of generating safety-based test cases

parses the XML specifications of the STPA project and Stateflow model into the corresponding Java objects by using Java Architecture for XML Binding (JAXB) technology. We implemented a Java library called SMV Generator which contains all necessary methods for transforming the XML specifications of the STPA project and Stateflow model into an SMV model. To check the correctness of the generated model against the LTL formulae of STPA software safety requirements, STPA TCGenerator uses the binary files of the NuSMV model checker to verify the generated SMV model. The process of generating safety-based test cases is shown in figure 6.8.

After validating the correctness of the safe behavioral model, the STPA TCGenerator generates a hierarchical tree of the safe behavioral model which shows the hierarchy levels of the safe test model. The *STPA TCGenerator* tool parses the tree of the safe behavioral model recursively by considering superstate decomposition *AND_STATE* (parallel) or *OR_STATE* (exclusive) to automatically generate the safe test model as an extended finite state machine. The tool automatically generates the traceability matrix between STPA software safety requirements and the safe behavioral model and shows them in a table. All input data variables with their data type, initial, minimum, maximum values which are shown in the test input configuration view.

Before running the tool to generate the test cases, the safety tester has to set the number of test steps, select the test coverage criteria (state, transition and STPA software safety requirements test coverage criteria). Furthermore, the safe tester has also to set the test input value for each input data variable of the safe

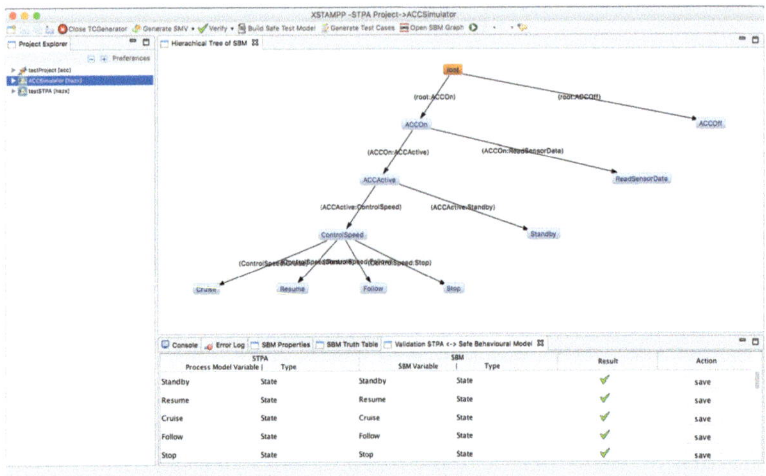

Figure 6.9.: STPA TCGenerator tool as an Eclipse-plugin in XSTAMPP

behavioral model. The tool automatically generates the safety-based test cases and show the measures of the test coverage and traceability matrix between the generated safety-based test cases and STPA-generated safety requirements. The results of STPA TCGenerator are automatically saved into CVS sheets.

To allow the safety tester to generate safety-based test cases directly in XSTAMPP platform, we developed an Eclipse-plugin for the STPA TCGenerator tool (shown in Figure 6.9). The STPA TCGenerator plugin version enables software and safety engineers to identify safety requirements of software by applying STPA to specification and design models and generate safety-based test cases from the STPA to measure the safety of the software implementation.

The first prototype of the *STPA TCGenerator* standalone version and the results of the illustrative example are available online in our repository[1]. The updatesite of the STPA TCGeneratorPlugin are available online in our repository [2].

[1] `https://sourceforge.net/projects/stpastgenerator/`.
[2] https://sourceforge.net/projects/stpatcgeneratorplugin/

6.1.3.5. A-CAST

A-CAST[1] (Automated CAST) [AW16] is an Eclipse plug-in tool which is developed based on the XSTAMPP architecture to support performing the CAST accident analysis steps and to help the analyst during investigating an accident based on the STAMP model. This tool does not support the STPA SwISs approach, but it was developed only to support the application of CAST accident analysis.

The CAST accident analysis approach has the following main steps [Lev11]:

- Identify the basis of analysis e.g. system-hazards which are violated, the system safety design constraints and proximal events.
- Construct the safety control structure as it was designed to work.
- Accident analysis in which the analyst should evaluate each component in the safety control structure diagram and determine whether it fulfilled its responsibilities or provided inadequate control. The analyst should also examine the coordination and communication between the main players of the accident under analysis.
- Edit recommendations.

A-CAST implements the aforementioned steps of CAST. It allows the safety analyst to draw the control structure diagram and document the safety responsibilities and roles of each component in the control structure diagram. Moreover, A-CAST allows the safety analyst to edit and document recommendations for each component directly on the control structure diagram by double-clicking on the component. The results of the CAST accident analysis can be exported completely in one PDF file or individually as PDFs, images, and CVS files for each CAST step. Figure 6.10 shows the main views of A-CAST in XSTAMPP.

[1]http://www.xstampp.de/a-cast.html

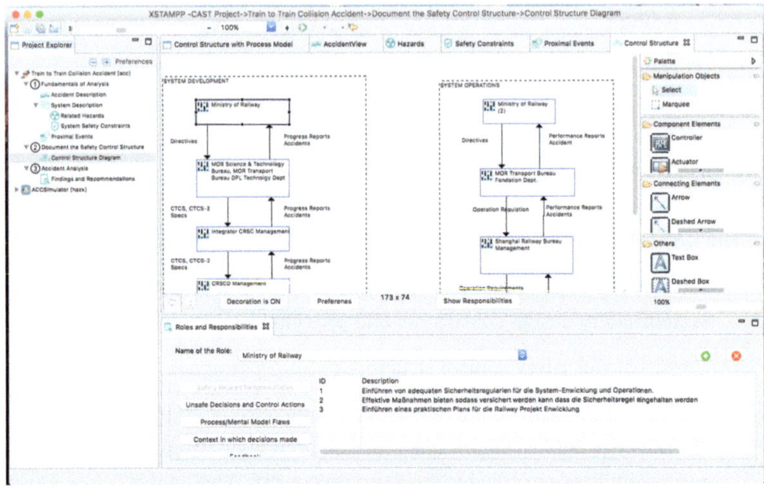

Figure 6.10.: The main view of A-CAST in XSTAMPP

6.2. Summary

We presented a tool support, called XSTAMPP which is developed to support the safety engineering approach for software-intensive systems. XSTAMPP supports the application of STAMP methodologies in different industrial environments. It also aims at implementing the steps of STAMP/CAST to support accident analysts in performing the STAMP/CAST method. Moreover, XSTAMPP provides a tool support to generate the context tables and to generate the corresponding formal specifications of the refined safety requirements to support the safety verification activities. XSTAMPP has different Eclipse plugins which are developed to support safety and software engineers in performing STPA safety analysis for software components at the system level, verify their software design and implementations against the STPA-generated safety requirements. XSTAMPP also allow the safety engineers to automatically generate safety-based test cases directly from the STPA results.

CHAPTER 7

EMPIRICAL VALIDATION

> *Empirical explorations ultimately change our understanding of which questions are important and fruitful and which are not.*
>
> — LAWRENCE M. KRAUSS

In this chapter, we describe the empirical validation of the STPA SwISs approach. STPA SwISs is an STPA-based approach for software safety, which can be applied during the development process of a new safe software or to an existing safety-critical software. Therefore, to explore its application during the development process of a new safety-critical software in terms of identifying the software safety requirements, verifying them and generating safety-test cases, we conducted a pilot case study on developing a safe software simulator of the adaptive cruise control system with a stop-and-go function. Moreover, we explore the application of STPA SwISs to real software systems by conducting two industrial case studies based on the automotive software systems. The first case study was conducted on the Active Cruise Control System (ACC) at BMW Group. The second industrial case study was conducted on the fully automated vehicle project at Continental.

7.1. Pilot Case Study: Developing A Software Simulator for ACC

7.1.1. Case Study Description

Adaptive Cruise Control (ACC) is a well-known automotive system which has strong safety requirements. ACC [SAE03] is an advanced version of the cruise control which allows a vehicleś cruise control autonomously adapt the vehicleś speed to the traffic environment. The operation of an ACC is based on a long

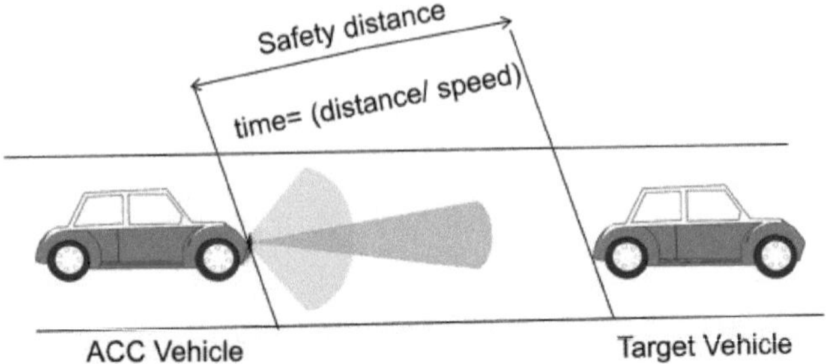

Figure 7.1.: A mechanism of the simulator of ACC with stop-and-go function

range forward-radar sensor which is attached to the front of the vehicle to detect whether there is a vehicle moving in the ACC vehicleś path. When the radar sensor detects a foregoing slow moving vehicle in the path, the ACC system will adapt the speed of ACC vehicle automatically (slow down or accelerate) and control the distance between the ACC vehicle and the target vehicle. If the road is free and the radar sensor detects that the target vehicle is no longer in the path, then the ACC will automatically return back the vehicle speed to its pre-set speed.

To illustrate the proposed approach, we developed a simulator software written in ANSI-C to simulate the *Adaptive Cruise Control Systems* system with stop-and-go function by using two LEGO EV3 Mindstorm robots[1]. We developed the simulator within 6 months (see the appendix A). The ACC with stop-and-go function [VN00] is an extended version of the normal adaptive cruise control system. It maintains a certain speed and keeps a safe distance from the vehicle ahead based on the radar sensors. The ACC with stop-and-go function will bring the vehicle to a complete stop when the vehicle ahead comes to a standstill or there is a stationary object in the lane.

Figure 7.1 shows the mechanism of the simulator of the ACC with stop-and-go function. The ACC simulator maintains a constant time gap to vehicles ahead. It

[1] http://www.iste.uni-stuttgart.de/en/se/forschung/werkzeuge/acc-simulator.html

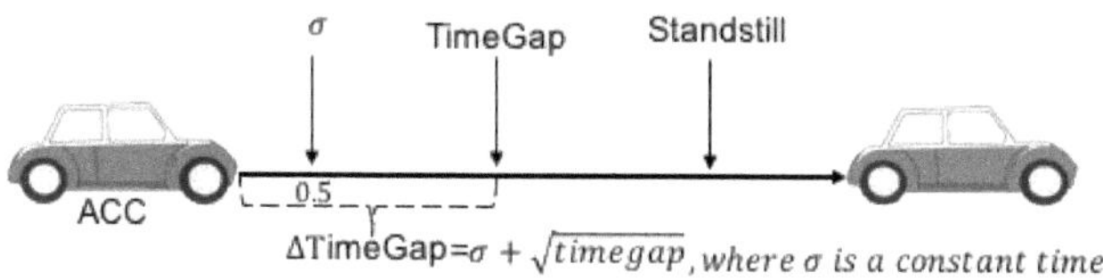

Figure 7.2.: The ACC system with stop-and-go function scenarios

uses a forward ultrasonic sensor with a range of up to 255 centimeters, which is located in the front of the robot to detect the distance of the robot ahead of it and can automatically maintain the pre-set time gap. It adjusts the robot speed by increasing or decreasing the value of current speed to keep a safe distance. If the robot ahead is completely stopped, then the ACC simulator will slow down the robot vehicle to a standstill. If the vehicle ahead starts moving again, then the ACC simulator will automatically start to move again and maintain a constant time gap between the robot ahead. Our simulator algorithm is the ACC simulator starts first read the distance data from the ultrasonic sensor and then computes the time gap by using the following equation:

$$currentTimegap = |\frac{Frontdistance}{CurrentSpeed}| \tag{7.1}$$

Second, the simulator computes the standstill time, which is the time at which the ACC vehicle must decrease the speed or stop when the vehicle ahead is close or fully stopped. It is calculated as

$$\Delta Timegap = stillstandtime + \sqrt{currentTimegap} \tag{7.2}$$

Third, the simulator will compare the value of the time gap with the following scenarios (shown in Fig. 7.2):

- *TimeGap > (ΔTimeGap + safeTimeGap).* This indicates that the vehicle ahead is so far from the point t_σ. The simulator will accelerate the speed of the vehicle robot till the desired speed. The simulator adjusts (increase/decrease) the current speed by using the following equation:

$$currentSpeed + /- = \sqrt{speed^2 + 2 * (Time)}, \tag{7.3}$$

where $Time = ((\Delta Timegap + safeTimeGap) - TimeGap)$

- *(TimeGap > safeTimeGap)* && *(timeGap < (ΔTimeGap + safeTimeGap))*. This indicates that the vehicle robot ahead is approaching within the period of time gap between $[t_\sigma \ t_{safeTimeGap}]$. The simulator will put the ACC system in *follow* mode. *Follow* mode means that there is a vehicle in front in the lane. The simulator will automatically adjust the current speed by using equation refeg:7.5.
- *TimeGap == safeTimeGap*. This indicates that the vehicle robot ahead is approaching within the desired time gap and there is a safety distance between them. The simulator will put the ACC system in the cruise mode. *Cruise* mode means that the vehicle robot ahead is approaching in safe time gap. Then, the simulator will set the current speed as the desired speed.
- *TimeGap < safeTimeGap*. This indicates that the vehicle ahead is moving within the time between $[t_{safeTimeGap} \ t_0]$. The simulator will reduce the speed of the vehicle by using equation 7.3.
- *TimeGap == 0*. This indicates that the vehicle ahead has fully stopped. Then the simulator will bring the vehicle to a complete stop at the standstill distance and change the ACC mode to stop. If the front vehicle starts to move again, then the simulator will change the ACC mode to resume. *Resume* mode means that the current speed of the ACC vehicle will be accelerated to the desired speed. The simulator uses the following equation to achieve that:

$$currentSpeed += accelerationratio, \tag{7.4}$$

where accelerationratio is set to 4 cm/sec;

7.1.2. Results

7.1.2.1. Deriving Software Safety Requirements of the ACC Simulator

To derive the software safety requirements, we applied the STPA SwISs Step 1 to the system specification requirements. We used the XSTAMPP software tool to document the results of STPA and generate the formal specification of the STPA results.

As a result, we identified the system-level accidents that the simulator software can lead (or contribute to). For example, **ACC-1 : The ACC robot crashes the robot ahead**. The system-level hazards which can lead to this accident are:

- H_1: The ACC software does not keep a safe distance from the a vehicle robot ahead.
- H_2: The ACC software provides an unintended acceleration when the vehicle in front is too close.
- H_3: The ACC software does not stop the vehicle when the vehicle ahead is fully stopped.

We built the control structure diagram of the ACC simulator (shown in Fig. 7.3). It contains the main interconnecting components of the ACC simulator at a high level, such as the *ACC simulator software controller unit, the electronic motors, the robot vehicle* as the controlled process, and *the Ultrasonic and speed sensors*. The ACC software controller receives the distance data from the ultrasonic sensor and current speed data from the speed sensor. Based on this information, the software will calculate the time gap and determine if the vehicle robot ahead is present. The ACC software will adjust the speed of the robot based on the above sensors and issues one of the critical safety control action: accelerate, decelerate, or fullystop. Each one of these control actions will be evaluated based on the four general hazardous types (columns of table 7.1). Table 7.1 shows the examples of the potential unsafe control actions of the ACC simulator.

We evaluated each item in table 7.1 to check whether it can contribute or lead to any system-level hazards (H_1– H_3). If an item is hazardous, then we assign one or more system-level hazards to it. We translate each hazardous item manually to the corresponding software safety requirement by using the guide

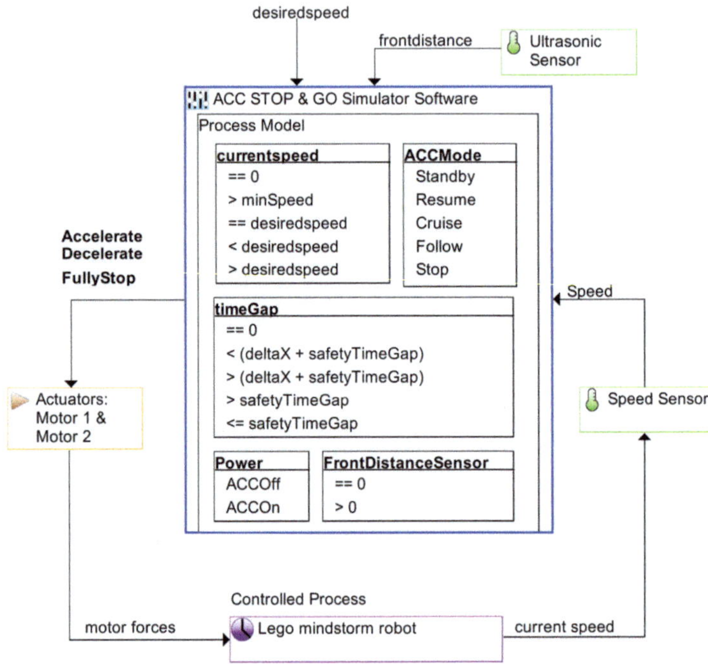

Figure 7.3.: The control structure diagram of ACC with the safety-critical process model variables

words, e.g., *shall or must be*. Table 7.2 shows examples of the informal textual software safety requirements.

To refine the informal textual software safety requirements which are shown in table 7.2, we identified the process model of the ACC software controller and its critical variables which have an effect on the safety of the ACC software control actions. Figure 7.3 shows the control structure diagram and process model variables of the ACC software. The ACC software has three safety-critical process model variables: *Internal variables* such as currentSpeed (5 values), Timegap (5 values), *Internal states variable* such as ACC mode (states) with 5 values, and *the environmental variables* such as front distance. Each safety

Table 7.1.: Examples of potentially unsafe control action of the acceleration control action

Not providing causes hazard	Providing causes hazard	Wrong timing or order causes hazard	Stopped too soon or Applied too long
The ACC software does not accelerate the speed when the robot vehicle ahead is so far in thelane. [**Not Hazardous**]	**UCA-1.1**: The ACC software accelerates the speed of robot unintendedly when the time gap to the robot vehicle ahead is smaller than the desired time gap. [**H-1**] [**H–2**]	**UCA-1.2**: The ACC software accelerates the speed before the robot vehicle ahead starts to move again. [**H-1**] [**H-2**]	**UCA-1.3**: The ACC software accelerates the speed too long so that it exceeds the desired speed of the robot. [**H-2**]

control action provided by the ACC software should be evaluated to determine whether it will be hazardous or not when the combination set of relevant values of the process model variables (context) occur.

We used XSTAMPP/XSTPA to generate the critical combinations (context tables) for each safety-critical action in the two contexts *when the control action is provided* and *it is not provided* and causes hazard. For each control action, the total number of combinations between the process model variables is ($5 \times 5 \times 5 = 125$) combinations. We reduced the number of combinations by applying pairwise test coverage to the generated combination sets. The number of critical combinations is reduced to 25 for each control action. Table 7.3 shows examples of the context table of providing the control action *accelerate* based on the combinations of the values of the critical process model variables. As a result, we identified 32 unsafe scenarios (shown in Table 7.4) for all the control actions *accelerate (18 scenarios)*, *decelerate (7 scenarios)* and *FullyStop (7 scenarios)*. Table 7.5 shows the examples of generated software safety requirements for the unsafe scenarios.

Based on the rules 3-4, XSTAMPP also automatically generates the LTL formula for each refined software safety requirement. Table 7.6 shows the examples of

Table 7.2.: Examples of corresponding safety constraints at the system level

Related UCAs	Corresponding Safety Constraints
UCA-1.1	**SSR1.1**- ACC software must not accelerate the speed of the robot when the target robot vehicle is too close in the lane.
UCA-1.2	**SSR1.2**- ACC software must not accelerate the speed when the robot ahead is fully stopped.
UCA-1.3	**SSR1.3**-ACC software must not increase the speed than the desired speed.
UCA-1.4	**SSR1.4**-ACC controller must stop the robot at standstill point (shown in Fig. 7.2) when the robot ahead is fully stopped.

Table 7.3.: Examples of the context table of *providing* the control action *accelerate*

Control Actions	Process Model Variables			hazardous Control Action?
	CurrentSpeed	TimeGap	ACC Mode	providing
accelerate	CS>minSpeed	TimeGap<(Δ Timegap + safety-TimeGap)	follow	No
	CS<= desired-Speed	TimeGap == 0	follow	Yes, H2, H1
	CS<desiredSpeed	TimeGap > safety-TimeGap	follow	No
	CS<desiredSpeed	TimeGap <(Δ TimeGap + safety-TimeGap)	follow	Yes

Table 7.4.: Examples of refined unsafe control action generated in XSTAMPP based on the results of STPA Step 1

ID	Unsafe software safety scenarios
RUCA-1.1	The ACC software controller provides the accelerate command when ACC mode is Standby and timeGap is greater than (deltaX + safetyTimeGap) and the current speed is less than desired speed.
RUCA-1.2	The ACC software controller provides the accelerate command when timeGap is less than (deltaX +TimeGap).
RUCA-1.3	The ACC software controller provides the accelerate command when current speed is greater than or equal to desired speed.
RUCA-1.4	The ACC software controller does not provide the fullyStop command when the timeGap is 0.
RUCA2.1	The ACC software controller provides the decelerate command too late when ACC mode is follow and timeGap is less than safetyTimeGap and currentSpeed is greater than desired speed.

the corresponding LTL formula of each software safety requirement. We used the generated-LTL formulae to verify the safe behavioral model which is constructed from the STPA results.

7.1.2.2. Automatically Generating SMV Model

We visualised the process model of the ACC software controller (shown in Fig. 7.3) by creating a Simulink/Matlab Stateflow model (shown in Fig. 7.4). The Stateflow contains 9 states (2 of them are superstates) and 19 transitions. It shows the relationship between the process model variables in the safety control structure diagram of the ACC simulator. The process model describes the critical variables and states of the software and how the software issues the critical safety control actions (e.g. accelerate, decelerate)

To validate the correctness of the safe behavioral model, we generated the SMV model of the safe behavioral model (shown in Fig. 7.4) by using the

Table 7.5.: Examples of refined software safety requirements

Related UCAs	Refined Safety Constraints
RUCA-1.1	**RSSR1.1**- Accelerate command must not be provided when ACC mode is Standby and timeGap is greater than (deltaX + safetyTimeGap) and the current speed is less than desired speed.
RUCA-1.2	**RSSR1.2**- Accelerate command must not be provided when timeGap is less than (deltaX +TimeGap).
RUCA-1.3	**RSSR1.3**-Accelerate command must not be provided when current speed is greater than or equal to desired speed.
RUCA-1.4	**RSSR1.4**-FullyStop command must be provided when the timeGap is 0.
RUCA2.1	**RSSR2.1**- Decelerate command must not be provided too late when ACC mode is follow and timeGap is less than safetyTimeGap and currentSpeed is greater than desired speed.

STPA TCGenerator tool which transforms the safe behavioral model into a verification input of the NuSMV model checker. For that, we first derived the XML specifications of the Simulink's Stateflow model. Second, we took the XML specifications of both ACC simulator STPA file and the safe behavioral model as input to the STPA TCGenerator tool. The tool parses both files and generates the SMV model which maps all states, transitions and data variables, and LTL formulae of STPA software safety requirements of the safe behavioral model to SMV model specifications. The generated SMV model is shown in the appendix A.

We updated the default values of each input data variable which are declared in the generated SMV model (e.g. *initial speed (10.0), desired speed (45.0), initial frontdistance (150.0)*). The value of current speed will be calculated by using equations 5. The value of time gap will also be calculated by using equation 2. The STPA TCGenerator tool runs the NuSMV 2.6.0 model checking tool to verify the generated SMV model file. The NuSMV model succeeded in verifying the generated SMV model within 0.29 seconds and no further errors were reported. NuSMV consumed 42.10 megabytes to store 2.31828e+17 states and performed

Table 7.6.: Examples of LTL formulae of the refined software safety requirements at the system level

Refined SSRs	Corresponding LTL formula
RSSR1.1	**LTL1.1**- G((state==Standby)&& (timeGap> deltaX+ safetyTimeGap) && (currenSpeed < desiredSpeed) → ! (controlAction==Accelerate)).
RSSR1.2	**LTL1.2**- G((currentSpeed > desiredSpeed) && (TimeGap <(deltaTime+safetyTimeGap)) →! (controlAction==Accelerate).
RSSR1.3	**LTL1.3**- G((currentSpeed >=desiredSpeed) →! (ControlAction==stop) .
RSSR1.4	**LTL1.4**- G((timeGap==0) → *X* (controlAction==FullyStop).
RSSR2.1	**LTL.2.1**- G((state==Follow)&&(timeGap <safetyTimeGap) && (currentSpeed >= desiredSpeed) → !(controlAction==Decelerate))

2.97418e+09 transitions. As a result, all LTL formulae were satisfied and there is no counterexample generated because the safe behavioral model itself was built from STPA software safety requirements.

7.1.2.3. Safety-based Test Case Generation

After validating the correctness of the safe behavioral model, we used the STPA TCGenerator to generate a hierarchical tree of the safe behavioral model which shows the hierarchy levels of the safe test model. The *STPA TCGenerator* tool parses the tree of the safe behavioral model recursively by considering superstate decompositions *AND_STATE* (parallel) and *OR_STATE* (exclusive) to generate the safe test model as an extended finite state machine. As a result, the generated safe test model contains 7 states (after removing the superstates) and 32 transitions (after maintaining the transitions of superstates). The tool automatically generates the traceability matrix between STPA software safety requirements and the safe behavioral model.

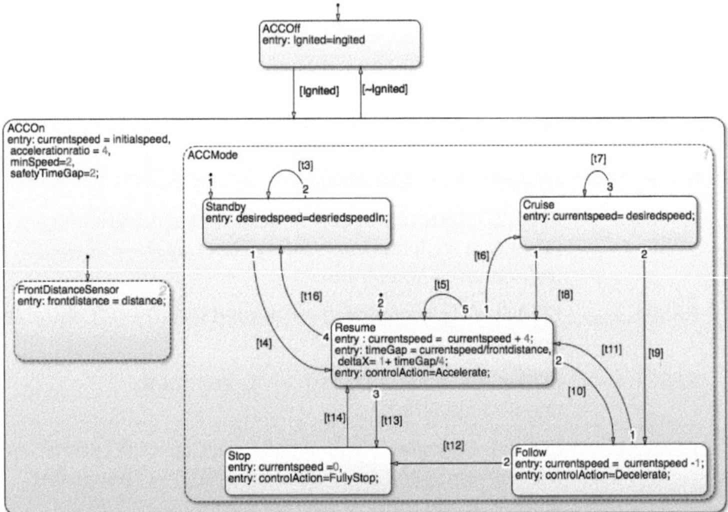

Figure 7.4.: The safe behavioral model of the ACC software controller

To generate the safety-based test cases from the safe test model of the ACC simulator, we first set the number of test steps to 10 and selected the three test coverage criteria (state, transition and STPA software safety requirements test coverage criteria) in the STPA TCGenerator tool. We selected the STPA software safety requirements coverage as the stop condition of the test case generating algorithm. We also set the test input value for each input data variable: *power* (true), desired speed (45 cm/sec), initial speed (10 cm/sec), front distance (150 cm). Finally, we ran the STPA TCGenerator tool three times to generate safety-based test cases from the test model, respectively: 1) depth-first search, 2) breadth-first search and 3) the combined algorithm. Table VIII shows the results of the generated safety-based test cases by each test algorithm. We could achieve 100% coverage of all the STPA software safe requirements which are linked to the safe test model in the traceability matrix. Figure 7.7 shows an example of the format of documenting each safety-based test case.

```
[Test Case ID] 2
[Test Suite ID] 2
[Related STPA SSRs]
   RSSR1.1, RSSR1.2, RSSR1.3
[PreConditons]
   desiredspeed=45.0
   frontdistance=120.32
   currentspeed=44.0
   state=Resume
[Actions]
   controlAction=Accelerate
[PostConditons]
   currentSpeed=45.0
   state=Cruise
[Comment]
```

Figure 7.5.: An example of a generated safety-based test case

Based on the traceability matrix between the model and the STPA software safety requirements, the *STPA TCGenerator* provides an *individual coverage* (how many test cases *TC* covered each *SSR*) by each test algorithm (shown in Fig. 7.6).

7.1.2.4. Verification of the ACC Software Source Code

To verify the software source code of ACC Simulator against the STPA-generated software safety requirements, we first generated the Promela model (see in Appendix A) by using STPA Verifier which includes the Modex 2.7 tool. Modex tool is for extracting the verification model directly from source code written in ANSI-C. The generated Promela model is shown in the appendix A. A few errors were in the generated Promela Model such as Modex does not include the C library *math.h* into the model. We traced all errors in the generated model to make it work correctly in SPIN. We configure SPIN 6.4.3 in STPA verifier plug-in using a depth of the search tree of more than 10^4. The SPIN model succeeded in verifying our software program within *1.38e+03* seconds and no further errors were obtained. SPIN consumed *1.1* gigabyte to store *7,642,219* states and performed *13333010* transitions.

Table 7.7.: The safety-based test cases generated by STPA TCGenerator tool

Test Algorithm	Test Steps	Test Suite	Test Cases	Time (in Sec)	State Coverage	Transition Coverage	STPA SRR Coverage
DFS	10	1	119	3	6/7= 85.7%	23/32= 71.9%	32/32= 100%
BFS	10	4	24	1	6/7= 85.7%	17/32= 53.1%	32/32= 100%
Both	10	5	249	2	7/7= 100%	18/32= 87.5%	32/32= 100%

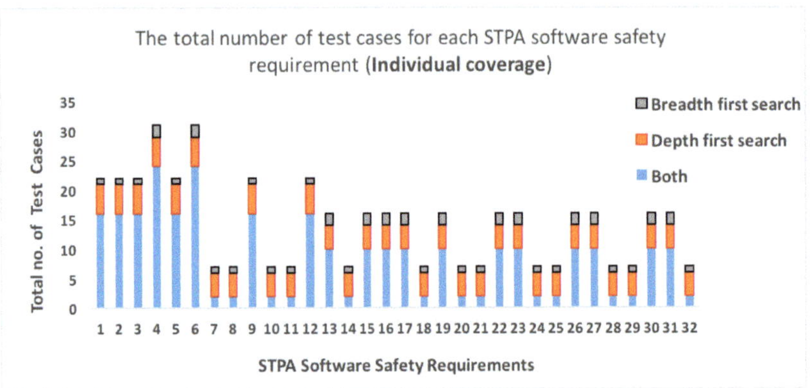

Figure 7.6.: The total number of test cases for each STPA software safety requirement

To verify STPA-generated safety requirements which are automatically expressed in LTL, we used STPA verifier plug-in which automatically generates the never claims for all LTL formulae by using the SPIN command line option. Next, STPA verifier included these never claims into the Promela model and ran SPIN to verify them one-by-one. Table 7.8 shows examples of the verification results of the software safety requirements with depth of search, number of different

Table 7.8.: Examples of the verification results of software safety requirements

SSR	#Depth	#States Stored	#Transitions	#Time (s)	#Memory (GB)	Results
SSR1.1	4964	9584017	16196785	1.5e+03	1.02	satisfied
SSR1.2	9999	8851830	15413578	1.4e+03	0.91	satisfied
SSR2.1	484	157289	294864	22.7	0.16	incomplete
SSR3.1	5	2	2	0.2	0.02	fails

states found in the model, number of transitions performed during depth-first search, total of memory needed for states and total time in second.

The results in table 7.8 show that the safety requirements SSR 1.1, SSR 1.2 and SSR 2.2 are satisfied while SSR 2.1 is incomplete because not all parts of the model were exercised. SSR 3.1 is refuted and a counterexample is yielded. To analyse the counterexample, we ran SPIN to perform a guided simulation using the trail file on the verification model. An example of SPIN result for this counterexample is shown as follows:

```
spin: trail ends after 5 steps
#processes: 10
5: proc 9 (p_main:1) model:701 (state 4)
5: proc 8 (p_runSimulator:1) model:623 (state 7)
5: proc 7 (p_radarSensorUnit:1) model:604 (state 7)
...
10 processes created
Exit-Status 0
```

The results show that the SSR3.1 fails because the radar unit monitor does not always provide *radarData* to the ACC software controller when ACC is in the cruise mode. This situation will cause an accident if there is a vehicle in the lane and the distance to a forward vehicle is too small. To eliminate this counterexample, we constrained the radar unit by checking the status of the ACC system before providing the data of the target vehicle.

7.1.3. Discussion

The idea behind the proposed approach is to integrate STPA safety analysis and its identification of the hazardous situations that the software can lead or contribute to semi-automatically with software testing. For this, we formalise the STPA software safety requirements into a formal specification and model the information derived from the STPA safety analysis into a test model. That helps us to focus the effort of testing by generating safety-based test cases for each software safety requirements. However, there are still some open issues and interesting challenges that require further research.

7.1.3.1. Visualisation of Process Model

The process model in the STPA control structure diagram is a very abstract model which shows only the safety-critical variables and states which have an effect on the safety of issuing the control actions by a software controller in the control structure diagram. It does not show how the software controller issues the control actions. Therefore, we use the statechart notation to visualise the relationships of the process model variables and describe the safe behavioral model. However, constructing a safe behavioral model from the STPA safety results by safety test engineers depends on the level of information which is available during the STPA safety analysis process (e.g. process model, and process model variables and values). Moreover, it is critical how this information describes the internal state of the software controller and the safety-critical software variables (e.g. interaction and environmental variables). Furthermore, visualising the safe behavioral model in a modelling tool such as Simulink requires user expertise in the modelling of dynamic behavior to map the safety analysis specifications (process model, control actions and software safety constraints) into the Stateflow notation. Therefore, this point remains as future work to automatically provide a basic structure of the safe behavioral model from the process model information (e.g. states and its hierarchical levels) which is visualised in XSTAMPP. This will help the safety tester to understand the relationships between the critical system states, environmental and interaction variables which are documented in the process model of the software controller in the STPA control structure diagram.

7.1.3.2. The Correctness of the Safe Test Model

The manual construction of test cases is a hard, time-consuming and error-prone activity that requires deep knowledge and expertise. Furthermore, the manual building of a test model from system specifications with the purpose of generating test cases still needs a proof of its correctness to ensure that the test model captures all specifications. A solution is to construct a test model for a given system and prove its correctness by transforming it into an intermediate model which is supported by a formal verification approach (e.g. model checker) to verify the generated model against its specifications. In addition, the specifications should also be mapped from informal text to the formal specifications. For this issue, we transformed the safe test model into the SMV model and verified it by using the NuSMV model checker to ensure that the safe test model satisfies the STPA specifications. However, the model transformation process also needs a proof of the correctness of the resultant model, even though the model checker did not induct any error. In our proposed approach, this issue remains as an open issue for future work.

7.1.3.3. Traceability Matrix

The automation of the test case generation process can lead to a large number of test cases that cover the same information. Reducing the number of generated test cases is a major factor in evaluating the effectiveness of an automated testing tool and the quality of the generated test cases. Therefore, we added a new test coverage criteria (STPA software safety requirements) to stop the test case generating algorithm when this criterion becomes 100% to ensure that each STPA safety requirement is covered at least in one test case. Furthermore, the first prototype of the *STPA TCGenerator* tool supports to generate test cases for each software safety requirement by automatically generating a traceability matrix by calculating the similarity degree of the matched tokens between the STPA software safety requirements and the safe test model. The traceability matrix contains all relevant transitions of each software safety requirement in the safe test model.

7.1.3.4. Process Model Variables Data Types

Another limitation is that the process model variables in the STPA control structure diagram visualised by XSTAMPP have no data types. Furthermore, XSTAMPP does not support multi-levels hierarchies of the process model of the software controller in the control structures. That makes ensuring and checking the consistency between the hierarchy levels of the process model in STPA and the Stateflow model in Simulink a big challenge. For example, the process model variable *ACC* Active in the *ACC* software controller has sub-process model variables such as control speed and *FrontDistancesensor* which will be activated when the ACC state is active. Therefore, it requires human effort to define the process model hierarchy and map it to the Simulink Stateflow model hierarchy level.

7.2. Industrial Case Study on BMW's ACC with Stop-and-Go function

7.2.1. Case Study Description

We conducted an industrial case study to explore the application of the *STPA SwISs* approach for safety engineering based on STPA using a real industrial system in the automotive domain. The case study was conducted at the German company BMW Group, which is a luxury automobile and motorcycle company. We applied the *STPA SwISs* approach to the BMW active cruise control system with stop-and-go function of the new car model G11. The case study was performed at the headquarters of BMW Group in Munich, Germany.

Figure 7.7 shows the case study work packages, deliverables and tool support. We started by applying STPA to the system specifications of ACC stop-and-go to derive the software safety requirements at the system level. We used XSTAMPP [AW15b] to document the results of applying STPA and transformed the STPA safety requirements automatically into formal specifications in LTL. Based on the results of STPA, we constructed a safe behavioral model of the ACC as a Simulink statechart. To ensure the correctness of the resulting model and STPA results, both are reviewed by two BMW experts. Furthermore, we automatically converted the safe behavioral model into SMV (Symbolic Model Verifier) [McM93] by using our tool *STPA TCGenerator* (STPA Test Case Generator)[1] which is a model-based safety testing tool. We also verified the SMV model against the STPA results by using the NuSMV model checker [Cim+00]. We used the safe behavioral model as input to our model-based testing tool *STPA TCGenerator* to generate safety-based test cases. Finally, we selected 20 of the generated safety-based test cases to be executed on the ACC system.

7.2.2. Case Study Design

In the following, we will describe the case study design which contains the main research questions that drive the case study, data collection and analysis procedures, as well as how we ensure the validity of the results. Our case study design follows Runeson and Höst's guidelines [RH08].

7.2.2.1. Study Goal and Research Questions

The goal of this case study is to explore the applicability and feasibility of the *STPA SwISs* approach of software safety engineering based on STPA in a real industrial environment. We use two research questions to structure the study design.

RQ1) How effective is using the *STPA SwISs* approach to derive the software safety requirements at the system level? This research question focuses on investigating how *STPA SwISs* helps to derive the appropriate software safety requirements at the system level to help the software and safety engineers to recognize the software risks.

RQ2) How useful is generating the safety-based test cases from the STPA results? We want by this research question to investigate how the safety-based test cases generated from STPA results can help to test the system against each software safety requirement to ensure that the system satisfies the STPA software safety requirements.

[1] `https://sourceforge.net/projects/stpastgenerator/`

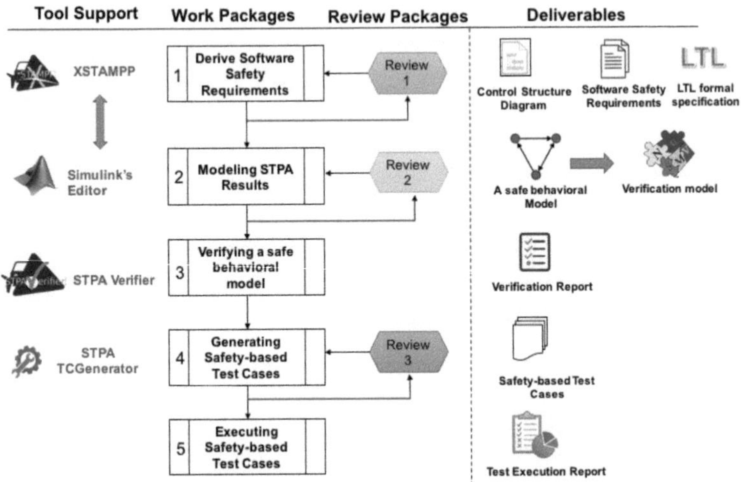

Figure 7.7.: Case study work packages, deliverables and tool support

7.2.2.2. Data Collection Procedures

The case study follows the 4 steps of the *STPA SwISs* approach to derive the software safety requirements and generate and execute the safety-based test cases on the system environment. Specifically, we apply the approach to the specification document of the active cruise control system with stop-and-go function. We use the XSTAMPP software tool to document the safety analysis results which are exported as PDF files and Excel sheets. We also use the reports generated by formal verification and testing approaches (e.g. STPA verifier and STPA TCGenerator). These reports include the verification results of each STPA safety requirement, the generated safety-based test cases and the test execution results.

7.2.2.3. Analysis Procedure

The following section describes the top-down process for applying the *STPA SwISs* safety engineering approach to the software controller of the active cruise control system in this case study:

Deriving the Software Safety Requirements: At first, the safety analyst investigates the existing documents about the case study object, its functional requirements, and its system specification. From these documents, the safety analyst establishes the fundamentals of the analysis (e.g. a list of the system-level accidents that the software can contribute to, a list of the system-level hazards that may lead to one or more of the system-level accidents) and builds a safety control structure diagram of the ACC system and its environment. The safety control structure diagram is a high-level abstraction diagram that contains the main components which interact with the ACC software controller and the necessary information about the input, software control actions and feedback signals. The control structure diagram is visualized by XSTAMPP. One of the internal ACC system designers reviews the control structure model and the STPA-generated software safety requirements and provides feedback to the safety analyst. Based on his feedback and improvement suggestions, the safety analyst modifies the diagram. The safety analyst uses the final control structure diagram to guide the safety analysis process to derive the software safety requirements based on the *STPA SwISs* approach.

Modeling of STPA results: Second, the safety and software engineers build a safe behavioral model of the software controller of the ACC system from the system specifications and STPA results. The safe behavioral model is a Simulink state chart model which contains the relevant process model variables (states) and transitions which is labeled by the STPA software safety requirements. The safe behavioral model was also reviewed by the ACC system designer and tester. The resultant model is reviewed by the ACC system testing expert at BMW.

Verifying the safe behavioral model: Third, the safety analyst transforms the safe behavioral model into the SMV (Symbolic Model Verifier) [McM93] specification model by using the *STPA TCGenerator* tool. Then the safety analyst verifies the SMV model against the STPA results by using the NuSMV model checker to ensure that the SMV model satisfies all STPA-generated software safety requirements.

Generating safety-based test cases: Fourth, the safety tester uses the XML specification of the safe behavioral model and the STPA project, which is created by XSTAMPP as input to the *STPA TCGenerator* tool to generate the safe model test and generate test cases for each STPA software safety requirement. The system tester determines the range of test data for each safety-critical variable (process model variable). The *STPA TCGenerator* tool automatically generates the traceability matrix between the software safety requirements and the safe test model and automatically generates the safety-based test cases from this model. The generated test cases are saved automatically in an Excel sheet. The generated safety-test cases are reviewed by the ACC testing expert at BMW.

Test execution of the safety-based test cases: Finally, we define criteria of selection safety-based test cases in which each generated software safety requirement should be tested at least in one test case. The safety analyst and system tester will conduct the execution of the test cases based on the final implementation of the ACC software system on the BMW car model series 7.

7.2.2.4. Measurements

To answer the research questions, we investigate the safety analysis and the verification and test case generation reports. Moreover, we investigate the execution results of the safety-based test cases.

To answer RQ1, we first summarise the results of deriving software safety requirements. We calculate the total number of the STPA-generated software safety requirements which are derived at the system level and the unsafe software scenarios which are reported by following *STPA SwISs* approach.

To answer RQ2, we investigate the list of the generated software unsafe scenarios to evaluate whether these scenarios describe real unsafe scenarios in the ACC system. We investigate the list of test cases generated and the execution testing report to evaluate how useful it is to generate test cases directly from the safety analysis. Finally, we calculate the coverage of the software safety requirements by the generated test cases generated by counting the total number of STPA-generated software safety requirements covered by safety-based test cases. We measure the Software Safety Requirements (SSR) coverage in the generated safety-based test cases by using the following equation:

$$\text{SSR Coverage} = \frac{|\#\text{STPA SSR covered by Test Cases}|}{|\#\text{STPA Software Safety Requirements}|} \tag{7.5}$$

7.2.2.5. Validity Procedure

To ensure internal validity, we define an extensive review role after each step. All generated software safety requirements, the control structure diagram of ACC, the safe behavioral model, the SMV model and the safety-based test cases are reviewed by the experts of the approach, the ACC system, and software and system safety. The experts provide valuable feedback and comments to ensure that all steps were conducted correctly and the results were obtained practically reasonable and acceptable.

An external validity concerns on how the proposed approach can be generalized to any software systems within the same industry or in a different industry. We perform a single case study with one company, nevertheless, we choose an automotive software of the well-known safety-critical system that has strong safety requirements. To ensure the external threat further studies on applying the *STPA SwISs* approach to different software systems in different industry domains are needed.

7.2.3. Results

In this section, we first present a detailed description of the case we selected. Then, we describe the results of the case study and answer the research questions.

7.2.3.1. Case Description

We carried out the case study on an automotive software system of the German company BMW Group. Active Cruise Control with stop-and-go (ACC) [1] (shown in 7.8) is an extended version of the adaptive cruise control system which keeps the vehicle at a safe distance from the vehicle in front at all times. It keeps

[1] `http://www.bmw.com/articles/active_cruise_control_stop_go.html`

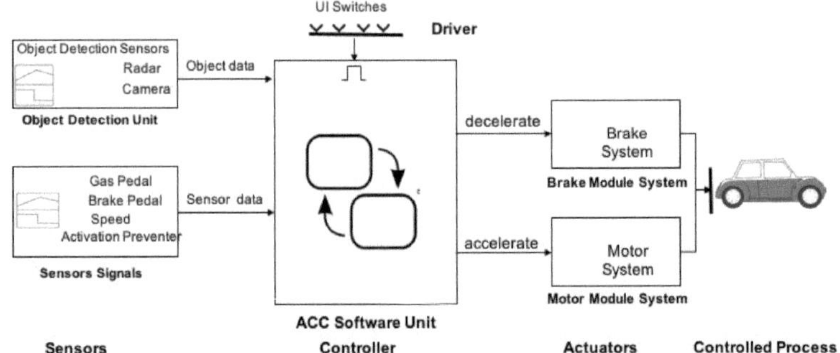

Figure 7.8.: The block diagram of BMW's ACC system with Stop-and-Go function

the vehicle speed constant within a range of 30 to 210 km/h and automatically adapts the following distance to the vehicle in front. The stop-and-go function controls the speed when the car slows down to a standstill and restarts the engine automatically after a short interval (< 3 seconds). When there is a traffic jam or the traffic comes to a halt, the ACC system with stop-and-go will apply the brakes until the vehicle comes to a standstill and then automatically will move on as soon as the road is clear.

7.2.3.2. Software Safety Analysis of BMW's ACC

Before applying *STPA SwISs* to the active cruise control system with stop-and-go function, we established the fundamentals of the analysis. We used the XSTAMPP tool to document the results of this step. Here we will summarise our results as follows: We identified 6 system-level accidents which the software of the ACC system can lead or contribute to (shown in Table 7.9). We also identified 9 system-level hazards which can lead to the accidents (shown in Table 7.10). We linked the system-level hazards to the accidents.

We drew the high-level safety control structure diagram of the ACC system (shown in Figure 7.9). The diagram shows the main components which interact with the ACC system. The main components of this diagram are: 1) ACC software as a controller component, which controls the controlled process (vehicle)

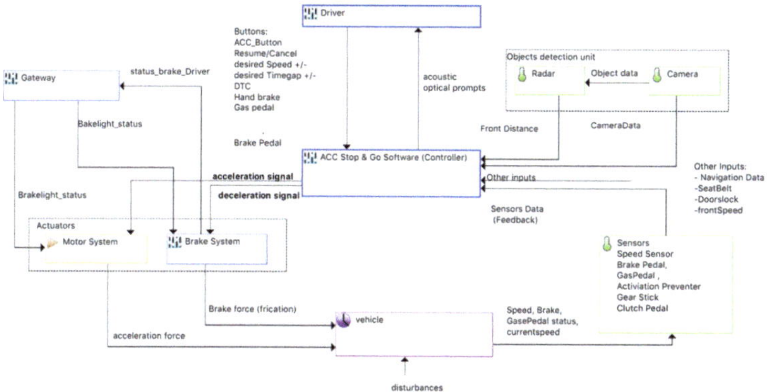

Figure 7.9.: The safety control structure diagram of the ACC system with Stop-and-Go function

by issuing control actions to the actuators; 2) The motor system and brake system are the actuator components which implement control actions of the ACC software controller; 3) The vehicle is the controlled process which is controlled by an ACC software control while the ACC system is active; and 4) a set of sensor components which send feedback about the status of the controlled process to the controller. The ACC software controller issues two safety-critical control actions: *acceleration signal* and *deceleration signal* to control the speed of the vehicle. We used this diagram to identify the potentially unsafe control actions of an ACC software controller in the ACC system.

We identified 21 unsafe control actions for the safety-critical control actions (shown in Table 7.11): *acceleration signal* (10 unsafe control actions) and *deceleration signal* (11 unsafe control actions). We evaluated each item in table 7.11 to check whether it can contribute or lead to any system-level hazards. If an item is hazardous, we assign one or more system-level hazards to it. Otherwise, we assign *not hazardous* to it. We translate each hazardous item manually to the corresponding software safety requirement. Table 7.12 shows examples of the informal textual software safety requirements.

To understand how each unsafe control action can occur and to identify the causal scenarios (causal factors), we identify the safety-critical process model

Table 7.9.: Examples of the system level accidents

ID	Accident	Description
1	ACC Stop & Go vehicle collides with a moving vehicle in the lane while the ACC system is active.	There is a vehicle moving slowly in the front of the ACC Stop & Go and the ACC vehicle does not reduce the speed or even bring a vehicle to the complete stop.
2	A vehicle is approaching too close behind the ACC Stop & Go vehicle and suddenly the ACC stop & Go vehicle is stopped without illuminating the brake light.	There is a vehicle is approaching behind the ACC Stop & Go vehicle and suddenly the ACC stop & Go vehicle is stopped while the vehicle behind is too close without illuminating the brake light.
3	ACC Stop & Go vehicle collides a stationary vehicle in the lane	There is a stationary vehicle in the front and ACC stop & go vehicle does not stop and ACC stop-and-go system is active.
4	ACC Stop & Go vehicle collides a small object (e.g. motorcycle) which is moving in the front	There is a small object such as a motorcycle or bike approaching in front of an ACC stop-and-go vehicle. The accident would occur if the object detection units (3 radar + camera) of the ACC stop-and-go could not recognize the small object.

variables of the ACC software controller (shown in Figure 7.9). The ACC software controller has a process model with 11 critical process model variables. These variables have an effect on the safety of the control actions. We classify the process model variables into three types of process model variables as follows:

- **Internal state variables** which indicate the internal states of the software controller of the system such as **ACCMode** which is a process model variable that indicates the status of ACC (active or inactive) and **states** which is a process variable indicating the operational modes of the ACC system. It has five states: *stop, standby, accelerate, cruise and decelerate.*

Table 7.10.: Examples of system level hazards

ID	Hazards	Accidents
1	ACC Stop & Go system does not keep a safe distance from a slowed-down object in front.	1,3, 4, 5
2	ACC Stop & Go system provides an unintended acceleration while the moving vehicle is too close.	1,3, 4
3	ACC Stop & Go system does not stop the vehicle when the traffic comes to a halt and the speed of the forward vehicle is zero (stationary).	3,4
4	ACC Stop & Go system does not keep a safe distance from the non-fixed objects in its lane.	5
5	ACC Stop & Go system does not maintain a safe distance from a small object (e.g. motorcycle) which is approaching in the front.	4
6	ACC Stop & Go system provides an unintended acceleration/deceleration that makes the vehicle uncontrolled in the critical situation.	4, 5, 6

- **Internal variables** which change the status of the controller such as **timeGap** which is calculated by an ACC software controller based on the front speed, current speed and front distance between the ACC vehicle and a vehicle in front of it and **currentSpeed** which indicates the current speed of the ACC vehicle.
- **Interaction Interface variables** which receive and store the data or command or feedback from the other components in the system such as *Brake status* which indicates the status of the brake pedal, *Gas Pedal* which indicates the status of the gas pedal, *resume_cancel button* which indicates the status of the resume_cancel button that actives ACC with last desired speed or deactivates ACC, *ACC button* which indicates the status of the ACC button, and the *Activation preventer* which is an aggregated variable that indicates the status of ACC activation preventer (e.g. driver belt, door lock, gear, etc.). The ACC activation preventer is a set of the ACC deactivation

Table 7.11.: Examples of potential unsafe control action *acceleration* of the ACC software controller

Not providing causes hazard	Providing causes hazard	Wrong timing or order causes hazard	Stopped too soon or applied too long
The ACC software controller does not provide the acceleration signal when the road is clear and the vehicle ahead is so far. **[Not Hazardous]**	**UCA1.1.** ACC software controller provides unintended accelerate signal when a slowed down object ahead is too close. **[H-1][H-2]**	**UCA1.3.** The ACC software controller provides an acceleration signal before the ACC is engaged and there is an object in the lane approaching too close. **[H-2]**	**UCA1.4.** The ACC software controller provides acceleration signal to motor unit too long which increases the current speed beyond the desired speed. **[H-6]**

Table 7.12.: Examples of corresponding software safety constraints at system level

UCA ID	ID	Corresponding Safety Constraints
UCA1.1	SR1.1	The ACC software controller must not provide an acceleration signal when a slowed down vehicle ahead is approaching too close.
UCA1.2	SR1.2	The ACC software controller must not provide an acceleration signal before the ACC system is engaged.
UCA1.3	SR1.3	The ACC software controller must increase the speed within the limit range of speed value (30 ...210 km/h).

variables. If the driver presses any ACC activation preventer button, then the ACC will be automatically deactivated or can not be activated.

We refine the unsafe control actions in table 7.11 based on the process model variables. First, we identify the dependencies between the control actions and the process model variables which have an effect on the safety of the control

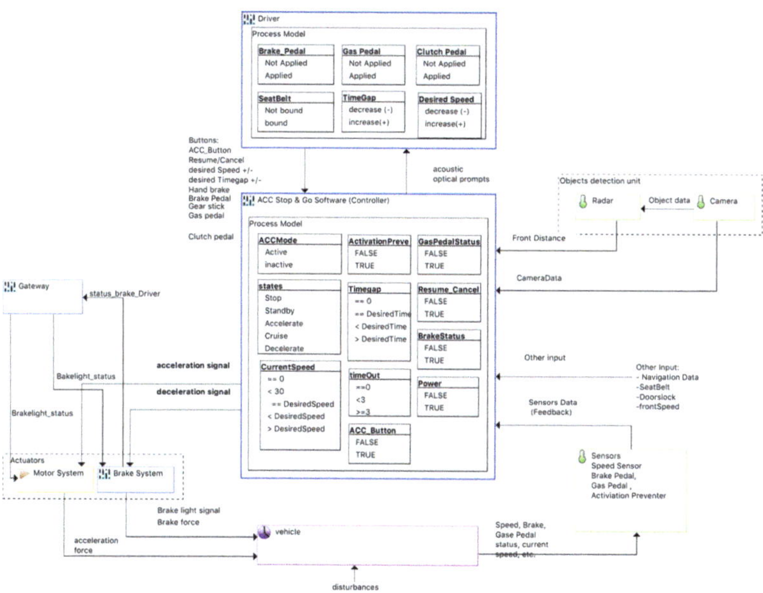

Figure 7.10.: The safety control structure diagram of the ACC system with the safety-critical process model variables

action to generate the context table for each control action (shown in Table 7.13).

Second, we identify the combination sets of relevant values of the process model variables (context) for each control action (shown in Table 7.14) to determine whether or not the control action in this context will be hazardous. We examine the combinations set in two contexts: *Provided control action causes hazard* and *Not Provided control action causes hazard*. The total number of all combination sets between the process model variables is calculated by the following equation:

$$\text{Total. No} = \text{Activation Preventer } x \text{ GasPedal } x \text{ states } x \text{ TimeGap } x \\ \text{CurrentSpeed } x \text{ BrakeStatus} \quad (7.6)$$

Table 7.13.: The dependency matrix between the control actions and the process model variables

Control Action	Relevant process model variables	Context
Acceleration Signal	Activation Preventer, Brake, CurrentSpeed, GasPedal, States, TimeGap	Provided/Not Provided
Deceleration Signal	Activation Preventer, Brake, CurrentSpeed, GasPedal, States, TimeGap	Provided/Not Provided

For the ACC stop-and-go software controller, the total number of all combination sets of process model variables is $= 2 x 2 x 5 x 5 x 6 x 2 = 1200$ combinations of process model variable values. To automatically generate the combinations and reduce their number, we used XSTPA[1] plugin in XSTAMPP which uses the combinatorial testing algorithm [KKL13] to automatically generate the context table and identify a minimal combination of process model variables for large and complex systems. XSTPA also automatically refines the unsafe control actions which are identified in STPA Step 1 and transforms the hazardous combinations in context tables into the LTL specifications.

To reduce the number of combination sets in XSTPA, we select the combinatorial testing algorithm (e.g. pairwise algorithm). The pairwise algorithm is a testing criterion which requires that for each pair of process model variables of the software controller, every combination of valid values of these two variables be covered by at least one combination set. The algorithm takes the two longest variable values. For example, the ACC stop-and-go software controller has the following process model variables: the *currentSpeed* (6 values) and *states* (5 values) are the two longest variables values. Based on that, we reduce the total number of combinations as $= 6 x 5 = 30$ combinations. Next, we generate the context tables with 30 combinations for each control action (acceleration, deceleration) in two contexts: *provided* and *not provided*.

[1] urlhttp://www.xstampp.de/XSTPA.html

Table 7.14.: Examples of the context table of providing the control action *acceleration signal*

Process model variables				Hazardous ?		
Activation preventer	States	CurrentSpeed	TimeGap	at any time	too early	too late
Off	Decelerate	>DesiredSpeed	Unknown	no	no	no
Off	Stop	Unknown	==0	yes	yes	yes
Off	Standby	Unknown	==DesiredTime	no	no	no
Off	Accelerate	>DesiredSpeed	<DesiredTime	yes	no	no
OffCruise		==DesiredSpeed	>DesiredTime	no	no	no

We use two strategies to generate the context tables and ignore irrelevant combinations:

- **Assumption 1:** We assume that the ACC system is active and all the sensors which make the ACC system automatically deactivate are off.
- **Assumption 2:** We assume that the ACC system is active and one of the sensors (e.g. brake pedal) which deactivates the ACC system is on.

Table 7.14 shows examples of the context table of providing the control action *acceleration signal*. The hazardous rules are automatically generated from the context table. We evaluated each hazardous rule and linked it to one or more unsafe control actions which are identified in STPA Step 1 to automatically refine the unsafe control actions with the process model variables and generate the refined software safety requirements. We identified 86 refined unsafe control actions for the ACC control actions. For example, the unsafe control action UCA1.1 ACC software controller provides unintended acceleration signal when a slowed down object ahead is too close can be refined as $RUCA$1.1: *ACC software controller provides the acceleration signal while ACC activation preventer is off, the brake pedal is not pressed, the state is stop, the gas pedal is not pressed, the current speed is unknown and time gap is ==0*. These 86 refined unsafe control actions are automatically transformed into the refined software safety requirements by our tool XSTAMPP/XSTPA. For example, the $RUCA$1.1 can be transformed

Table 7.15.: Examples of refined software safety constraints based on process model variables

RUCA	ID	Refined Software Safety Constraints	LTL
RUCA1.1	RSSR1.1	The ACC software controller must not provide an acceleration signal when the activation preventer is off, the state is Stop, the gas pedal is not pressed, the brake pedal is not pressed, the current speed is unknown and the time gap is equal 0 (traffic jam).	LTL1.1
RUCA1.2	RSSR1.2	The ACC software controller must not provide an acceleration signal when the activation preventer is off, the state is stop, the gas pedal is not pressed, the brake pedal is not pressed, the current speed is less than desired speed and the time gap is less than desired time.	LTL1.2
RUCA1.3	RSSR1.3	The ACC software controller must not provide an acceleration signal when the activation preventer is off, the state is Decelerate, the gas pedal is not pressed, brake pedal is not pressed, the current speed is greater than the desired speed and the time gap is less than the desired time.	LTL1.3

into the refined software safety requirement $RSSR1.1$ as *The acceleration signal must be not provided any time or too late or too early when activation preventer is off, the brake pedal is not pressed, the state is stop, the gas pedal is not pressed, the current speed is unknown and time gap is* $== 0$. Table 7.15 shows examples of the refined software safety requirements based on process model variables which were generated by XSTPA.

We also identified 123 causal scenarios that lead to the 21 unsafe control actions which are identified in the STPA Step 1 by analysing the control loops in the control structures diagram in Figure 7.10. For example, a causal scenario of the unsafe control action $UCA1.1$: *ACC software controller provides unintended accelerate signal when a slowed down vehicle ahead is too close.* is defined as

Table 7.16.: Examples of the causal scenarios of the unsafe control action UCA1.1

Unsafe Control Action (UCA1.1): The ACC Software controller provides an unintended acceleration signal when a slowed down object ahead is too close.

Refined Unsafe Control Action (RUCA 1.1): The ACC software controller provides an acceleration when the activation preventer is off, the ACC state is stop, the gas pedal is not pressed, the brake pedal is not pressed, the current speed is unknown and the timegap is equal 0

ID	Causal Scenarios	Safety Constraints
SC.1	The ACC software controller provides an acceleration signal while the ACC vehicle is stopped in a traffic (timegap=0) and there is a stopped vehicle in the front	The ACC software controller shall not provide an acceleration signal while the time gap between the ACC vehicle and the stopped vehicle in front is equal (to) 0.
SC.2	The ACC software controller provides an acceleration signal while the driver-seat belt (Activation preventer is on) is not bound (maybe the driver went outside the vehicle after waiting for a long time in the traffic jam)	The ACC software controller shall not provide an acceleration signal while the driver-seat belt is not bound.

$CS1.1$: *The ACC software controller receives incorrect data from radar in front which leads to wrong estimation of time gap while a vehicle ahead is too close.* Table 7.16 shows examples of the causal scenarios of the unsafe control action $UCA1.1$: *The ACC Software controller provides an unintended acceleration signal when a slowed down object ahead is too close.*

For each refined software safety requirement, an LTL formula will be generated automatically. For example, the LTL formula of the $RSSR1.1$ can be expressed as:

Table 7.17.: Examples of the corresponding LTL specifications of the software safety requirements

ID	LTL Formulas
RSSR1.1	[]((((ActivationPreventer==off) && (Brake==Notpressed) &&(States==Stop) && (GasPedal==NotPressed) && (CurrentSpeed==Unknown) && (TimeGap==0))→ !(controlAction==accelerationsignal))
RSSR1.2	[]((((ActivationPreventer==off) && (Brake==Notpressed) && (States==Accelerate) && (GasPedal==NotPressed) && (CurrentSpeed<DeisredSpeed) && (TimeGap<DesiredTime))→ !(controlAction==accelerationsignal))
RSSR1.3	[]((((ActivationPreventer==off) && (Brake==Notpressed) && (States==Decelerate) && (GasPedal==NotPressed) && (CurrentSpeed>DeisredSpeed) && (TimeGap<DesiredTime)) → !(controlAction==accelerationsignal))

$LTL1.1$ = [ ] ((ActivationPreventer==off && brake==off && states== stop && gaspedal=off && currentspeed==unknown && timegap==0) → ! (ControlAction==accelerationsignal)).

The LTL formulae will be used to verify the safe test model against the STPA results. Table 7.17 shows examples of the generated LTL formulae of the software safety requirements.

7.2.3.3. Modeling STPA Results

After deriving the software safety requirements of the ACC stop-and-go system, we created a Simulink/Matlab Stateflow model to visualize the STPA results with a safe behavioral model (shown in Figure 7.11). The safe behavioral model contains the process model variables of the ACC software controller (shown in Figure 7.10) and shows the relationship between the process model variables and hierarchy levels between the process model variables and its values. This model constraints the transitions between the process model based on the STPA results. The model contains 9 states (3 superstates and 6 sub-states) and 20 transitions.

7.2.3.4. Software Safety Requirements Verification

To check the correctness of the safe behavioral model which is constructed within Simulink's Stateflow against the STPA process model and the STPA-generated software safety requirements, we first used the Matlab command line to derive the XML specifications of the safe behavioral model of the ACC stop-and-go system. The XML specifications are saved in an XML file called *ACCStopandGo.xml*. Second, we used the *STPA TCGenerator* tool to automatically transform the safe behavioral model into the verification model in an SMV (Symbolic Model Verifier) model. The tool takes two input files: An STPA project of the ACC system which documents the results of step 1 and the XML specification file of the safe behavioral model. The tool will parse both files and generate the SMV model which maps all states, transitions, and data variables of the safe behavioral model and the LTL formulae of STPA-generated software safety requirements to SMV model specifications and automatically save them to a file named *ACCStopandGo.smv*.

To verify the generated SMV model against the STPA software safety requirements, we used the STPA verifier plug-in [1] which is an Eclipse plug-in to verify the STPA safety requirements with model checking tools such as SPIN and NuSMV. As a result, all LTL formulae of the STPA-generated software safety requirements are stratified except 5 of them are not stratified and counterexamples are generated. We updated the safe behavioral model based on the counterexample results and generated an updated SMV model. We verified the updated SMV model against the LTL formulae. Finally, all LTL formulae were stratified by the updated SMV model.

7.2.3.5. Safety-based Test Case Generation

To automatically generate safety-based test cases, we use the safe behavioral model which is constructed from the STPA safety analysis results and validated the STPA-generated safety requirement as input to *STPA TCGenerator*. STPA TCGenerator parses Simulink's Stateflow of the safe behavioral model recursively by considering Simulink's statechart notations (superstate decompositions

[1] `http://www.xstampp.de/STPAVerifier.html`

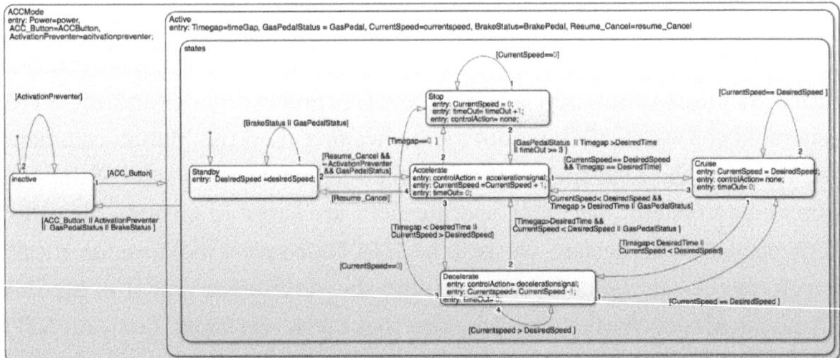

Figure 7.11.: The safe behavioral model of the ACC stop-and-go software controller

AND_STATE and OR_STATE) to automatically transform the statechart notations into the extended finite state machine notations to generate the safe test model. As a result, the safe test model contains 7 states (after removing the superstates) and 22 transitions (after maintaining the transitions of superstates by considering the state decomposition type). *STPA TCGenerator* automatically provides the traceability matrix between the STPA-generated software safety requirements and the safe test model. It also shows the input variables of the safe test model (e.g. currentspeed, timeOut, timegap, etc.) with their data type, initial, minimum, maximum values to allow the user to set the test input data and the test configuration.

We set the *STPA TCGenerator* with the test configurations as follows (shown in Figure 7.12): the number of test steps to 20; the test algorithm is the random walk with depth-first and breadth-first search; the test coverage criteria are the state-based, transition-based and STPA software safety requirements test coverage criteria; and the stop condition is STPA software safety requirements. We also set the input value for each test data variable: desiredspeed (30–210 kmh), deisredTimegap (2,4 seconds), Timegap (0–10 seconds), currentspeed(0–210 kmh), power (true), brakepedal (false–true), gaspedal (false–true) and Activation preventer (false–true).

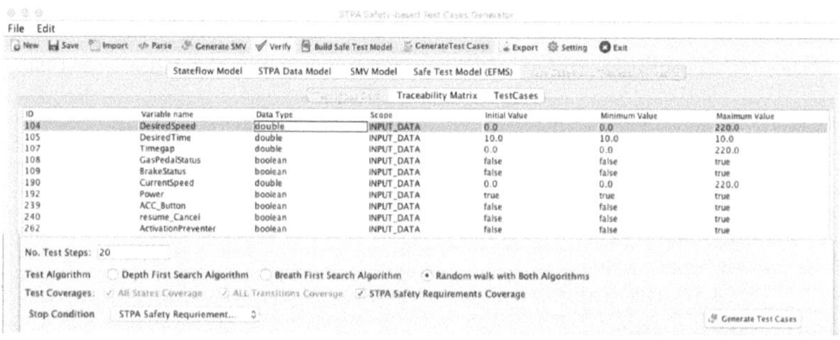

Figure 7.12.: The test configuration view in the STPA TCGenerator

As a result, we generated 40 test suites with a total of 230 test cases within 100.0% state coverage, 82.59% transition coverage, and 100 % STPA safety requirement coverage. 180 out of the 230 test cases are safety-based test cases which have a relation with one or more STPA safety requirements in the traceability matrix. The test cases are automatically saved in a CSV file.

7.2.3.6. Execution of the Safety-based Test Cases

Based on the available resources (time and hardware) from our industrial partner, we were allowed to execute only 20 test cases. We selected 20 test cases out of 180 which are more relevant for the critical control actions of the ACC software controller and the STPA-generated software safety requirements. We executed the selected test cases by driving the car on the highway. The safety analyst and system tester conducted the execution of the test cases on the BMW car model 7 series. They drove first from the university of Stuttgart to the highway because they could not perform the test in the city due to the safety reasons and the BMW car model was under test. The test was performed in a realistic environment on a German highway under cloudy weather. Table 7.18 shows the examples of the selected safety-based test cases with the execution results. As a result, the ACC stop-and-go system succeed with 18 out of 20 safety-based test cases. One test scenario was difficult to test. The test scenario was to test the stop function when there is a traffic jam and the vehicle in front moved slowly. As a requirement, the ACC stop-and-go will automatically restart the

Table 7.18.: Examples of the selected test cases and the test execution results

#No.	#Precondition	#Post-condition	Road status	#Test Result
1	currentspeed=100 DesiredSpeed=83 DesiredTimeGap=2.4 TimeGap>=2.4 Gaspedal=true Brakestatus=false Power=true ACC_Button=false Resume_Cancel=false ActivatPreven.=false currentstate=Accelerate	controlAction= accelerationsignal State= Accelerate	No vehicle in the lane	Success
2	currentspeed=0 DesiredSpeed=70 DesiredTimeGap=2.4 TimeGap=0.0 Gaspedal=false Brakestatus=true Power=true ACC_Button=false Resume_Cancel=false ActivatPreven.=false currentstate=stop timeOut=1.0	controlAction= none State= Stop	A vehicle in front in the lane	incomplete

engine and move off the vehicle, if the stop lasts from 1 to 3 seconds, otherwise it will automatically stop the vehicle until the vehicle in front starts moving again. For this situation, we used a timer to calculate the time of the stop. But it was difficult to measure the stop time of the vehicle in front within 1 or 2 seconds and move again. In another test scenario, we recognized that if the ACC stop-and-go is in the deceleration state (currentspeed > desired speed and there is a vehicle is in front) and the driver pressed on the ACC button, then the vehicle speed is immediately decelerated too slowly.

7.2.4. Discussion

Table 7.19 summaries all results of the case study. Based on the results of the case study, we answered our research questions as follows: For research question RQ-1, we identified 6 system-level accidents to which the ACC software can contribute to and 9 system-level hazards. We also identified 21 unsafe control actions. Furthermore, we identified 86 refined unsafe scenarios that describe different hazardous events that the ACC software transits the ACC system into hazardous behaviors. We automatically identified 86 refined software safety requirements based on the process model variables of the control actions of the ACC software controller: *acceleration and deceleration signals*. We also identified 123 causal scenarios that the ACC software controller can contribute to. The evaluation of *STPA SwISs* substantiates that: 1) the STPA-based analysis approach help us to identify the hazardous situations of the ACC software controller at the system level and develop detailed software safety requirements; 2) and it help us to transform the informal software safety requirements into formal specification in LTL to be used for the verification purpose.

To investigate research question RQ-2, the results reveal that we could generate 180 safety-based test cases from the results of research question RQ-1. All software safety requirements which are identified in step 1 are covered in at least one safety-test case. We obtained 100% for the Software Safety Requirements (*SSR*) coverage in the generated safety-based test case. That means we can test the ACC system against each software safety requirements with different test cases to measure the safety of the whole system. Deriving test cases directly from the safety analysis results allows us to focus the testing effort to test the critical risky situations. We were able only to execute 20 out of 180 safety-based test cases, however, we could recognize different situations of ACC software behaviors.

As a limitation, we could only execute a few generated safety-based test cases. Furthermore, we were not able to test some of the test scenarios to recognize some of the unsafe behaviors such as a bicycle moving in front of the ACC vehicle in the lane or a small stationary obstacle in the lane.

Table 7.19.: A summary of the case study results

ID	Item	Total. No
1	System Level Accidents	6
2	System level Hazards	9
3	Unsafe control actions	21
4	Corresponding software safety constraints	21
5	Refined unsafe control actions	86
6	Refined software safety constraints	86
7	Causal factors	123
8	Generated LTL formulae	86
9	Generated test cases	230
10	Safety-based test cases	180

7.3. Industrial Case Study on Continental's Fully Automated Vehicle

The content of this section has been presented at the 4th European STAMP Workshop and published at Procedia Engineering Journal [Abd+16].

7.3.1. Case Study Description

Fully automated vehicles represent a major innovation in the automotive industry which will replace driver tasks by software functions to make traffic more comfortable. Ensuring the safety of the fully automated vehicles is a big challenge. However, demands on fully automated driving vehicles, like a fail operational and nominative performance, are not covered by the current automotive safety standards like ISO 26262 (Road Vehicle–Functional Safety) [ISOv] is an international functional safety standard that provides guidance, recommendation and argumentation for a safety-driven-product development in the automotive area. Safety classification and suggestions for specific safety development processes may aid to stipulate functional safety for each new product as state-of-the-art. These standards were not established for fully automated vehicles.

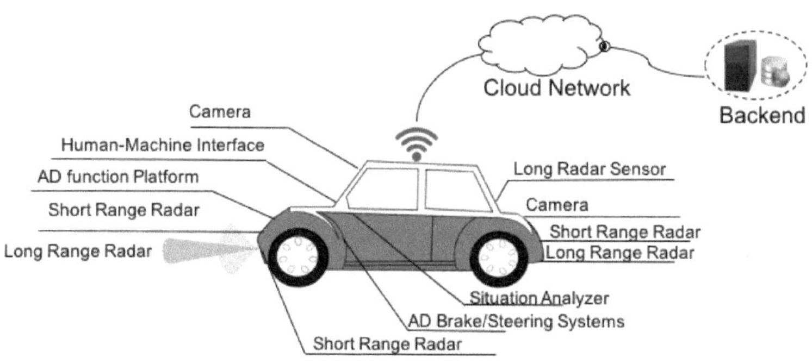

Figure 7.13.: A Fully Automated Driving Vehicle

Nowadays, innovations in software and technology lead to increasingly complex automotive systems such as self-parking vehicles, the use of smartphones to park vehicles and more recently fully automated driving vehicles. As a new technology, the fully automated driving vehicles may bring a new safety risk and threats to our society which have to be controlled during their development. Hence, the safety analysis becomes a great challenge in the development of safety-critical systems. In the past, failures of the automotive systems beyond separate component malfunction like interface problems led to safety issues. The automotive industry started to pay attention to the functional safety of vehicle electronic control systems and to have safety standards to address the growing complexity of its systems.

To explore the application of the STPA SwISs approach with complex software system, we applied *STPA SwISs* to the fully automated vehicle project at Continental to derive the software safety requirements and provide design recommendations to engineers to help them in assessing the fully automated driving architecture. This case study is conducted in the form of an industrial cooperation between the Institute of Software Technology at the University of Stuttgart and Continental to develop a safe architecture design for the current autonomous vehicles at Continental.

7.3.2. Fully Automated Vehicle

A fully automated vehicle (Figure 7.13) is highly reliant on software and vehicular networks to autonomously steer a vehicle on the road. Moreover, semi-automatic and fully automated driving system requires compliance with the essential system features such as reliability, availability, security and safety. A fully automated driving system (SAE Level 5)[1] involves the act of navigating the car without any input from the human driver through the use of sensing the environment, performing and calculating a desired driving path (trajectory) and sending the desired controls to the actuators. Therefore, the required components for a fully automated driving system can be classified in three main groups: 1) perception (sense), 2) Motion Planning (PLAN), 3) motion control , and 4) act. Figure 7.14 shows the functional architecture of the fully automated vehicle, which is divided into the following parts:

Perception (Sense) Observation of the vehicle surroundings by various sensors such as short and long-range radars, stereo cameras, mono cameras and lidar systems. Raw sensor output is either preprocessed (e.g. filtering, compression, pre-interpretation) by the sensor itself or sent directly to a unit for further processing. Data from different sources is merged by sensor fusion and interpreted, e.g. object recognition, traffic sign recognition, road and lane detection. Data fusion increases the reliability of the perceived environment by combining different sensor types. The environment model is an abstract representation of the perceived environment that uses structured data types to model all relevant elements. Localization of the ego vehicle is done by different means, e.g. GPS (Global Positioning System), SLAM (Self Localization and Mapping), Odometry and landmarks and lane markings. Ego position and motion are made available for functions.

Motion Planning (PLAN) Based on the environment model and ego position on the digital map, ego motion and mission goal (i.e. navigational instruction where to go) of the vehicle's desired trajectory is determined. The term Driving Strategy stands for higher-level behavior and maneuver planning (Driving

[1] http://www.sae.org/misc/pdfs/automated_driving.pdf

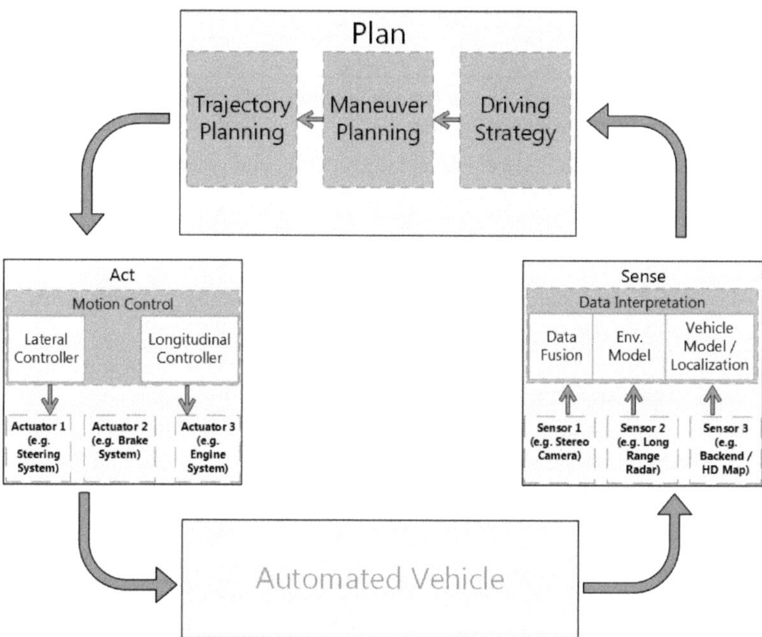

Figure 7.14.: Functional Architecture of the Fully Automated Vehicle at Continental [Abd+16]

Strategy). The resulting maneuvers are passed to trajectory planning which calculates an optimal, collision free trajectory to follow the desired maneuver reference. At the same time, the trajectory planner is a reactive layer, which can deviate from the reference by the driving strategy to avoid collisions or undesired vehicle states. During normal operation, the trajectory will follow the reference but will react to unpredicted situations, e.g. quickly decelerates when another car suddenly crosses the ego path unpredictably. The desired trajectory is a vector of points in the state space (position, time and motion) and represents the track that ego vehicle has to follow. The desired trajectory is passed on motion control.

Table 7.20.: Examples of the system level accidents

ID	Accident
1	Fully automated vehicle lost the steering and crashed into an object moving in front on highway.
2	Fully automated vehicle lost the steering and crashed into the ego lane.
3	Fully automated vehicle made an accident while an object suddenly is appeared in its lane in front.
4	Fully automated vehicle lost the steering/braking suddenly while the vehicle moving up in the hill and made an accident.
5	Fully automated vehicle made an accident due to fake data of sensors by an anonymous person.
6	Fully Automated driving vehicle made an accident due to loss the communication signals with backend.

Motion Control: Motion control has the task to perform lateral and longitudinal vehicle guidance along the desired trajectory. A longitudinal and a lateral controller produce control outputs to the vehicle actuators in order to keep the vehicle on the desired trajectory. Actuators heavily depend on vehicle type. For traditional passenger cars, these are e.g. engine control unit, electric steering, brake system and automatic transmission. The other vehicle types, e.g. robocabs or electric vehicle have different higher level interfaces which accept motion or steering commands and translate them into the corresponding suspension and steering types.

ACT: In the ACT subsection, all actuators (e.g. brake system, steering system and engine control) required for longitudinal and lateral movement, can be summarized. The output of the motion controller provides the torque requests for the actuators.

Table 7.21.: Summary of the identified hazards at the architectural level

Hazard Category	No. of Hazards	Linked Accidents
Road Surface Detection	4	1–12, 16 –19
Object Detection	23	1–13, 15–20
Control Hazard	47	1, 2, 12,15, 24-26
Localisation & Mapping	8	1–21, 24-26
Environmental Model	34	1–13, 14–21
Decision Making	30	1–21
Data Communication	10	1–19, 21
Individual ECU Defect	5	1-19
Security Attacks	15	20-23
Total	176	

7.3.3. Results

As the fully automated vehicle is a new project, we aimed to assess the architecture design of the fully automated vehicle by applying the STPA SwISs approach to the architectural design and specification to gain deep understanding of the unsafe scenarios of the fully automated vehicle. We summarised the results of applying STPA SwISs to the fully automated vehicle at the architectural level as follows:

7.3.3.1. Safety Analysis of Fully Automated Driving System

At first, we established the fundamentals of the analysis by identifying the system-level accidents and the associated hazards. As a result, we identified 26 system-level accidents which the fully automated driving can lead or contribute to (shown in Table 7.20). For example, *ACC1: Fully automated vehicle lost the steering and crashed into an object moving in front on highway.* Second, we identified the associated hazards which can lead to these accidents. We identified 176 hazards which are grouped into 9 categories (shown in Table 7.21). Table 7.22 shows examples of the system-level hazards. Next, we drew the high-level control structure diagram of the fully automated driving system

Table 7.22.: Examples of system level hazards

ID	Hazards	Category
1	The fully automated vehicle lost steering control while there is snow and Ice on road.	HG1. Road Surface Detection
2	The fully automated vehicle does not detect sings and marking of change the speed or direction or others.	HG.2 Object Detection
3	The fully automated vehicle provide a too high acceleration signal.	HG3. Control Hazard
4	The fully automated vehicle does not receive the map location data.	HG4. Localization & Mapping
5	The fully automated vehicle receive insufficient Environmental Model data.	HG5. Environmental Model
6	The fully automated vehicle moves with no maneuver planning	HG6. Decision Making

at the architectural level (shown in Figure 7.15). The control structure diagram includes: 1) the Fully automated Driving system (AD) as the main controller, which compresses a set of software control systems; 2) the motion control as an actuator; and 3) sense sensors (e.g. vehicle sensor, environmental model sensor, localization sensor, etc.).

The fully automated driving system issued the trajectory to motion control to steer the vehicle. The trajectory contains a time sequence of state-space points with **timestamp** (date/time on which the vehicle is to pass through the trajectory point), **global x position** (a position in the coordinate system), **global y position** (a position in the coordinate system), **trangente/track angle** (an angle of the given point), **curvature** (the amount by which a geometric object such as a surface deviates from being a flat plane or a curve), **curvature rate** (curvature changes over time), **velocity** (the speed of the vehicle for the given trajectory point), **acceleration** (acceleration of the vehicle at the given trajectory point), and **jerk** (the rate of change of acceleration; that is, the derivative of acceleration with respect to time, and as such the second derivative of velocity, or the third derivative of position).

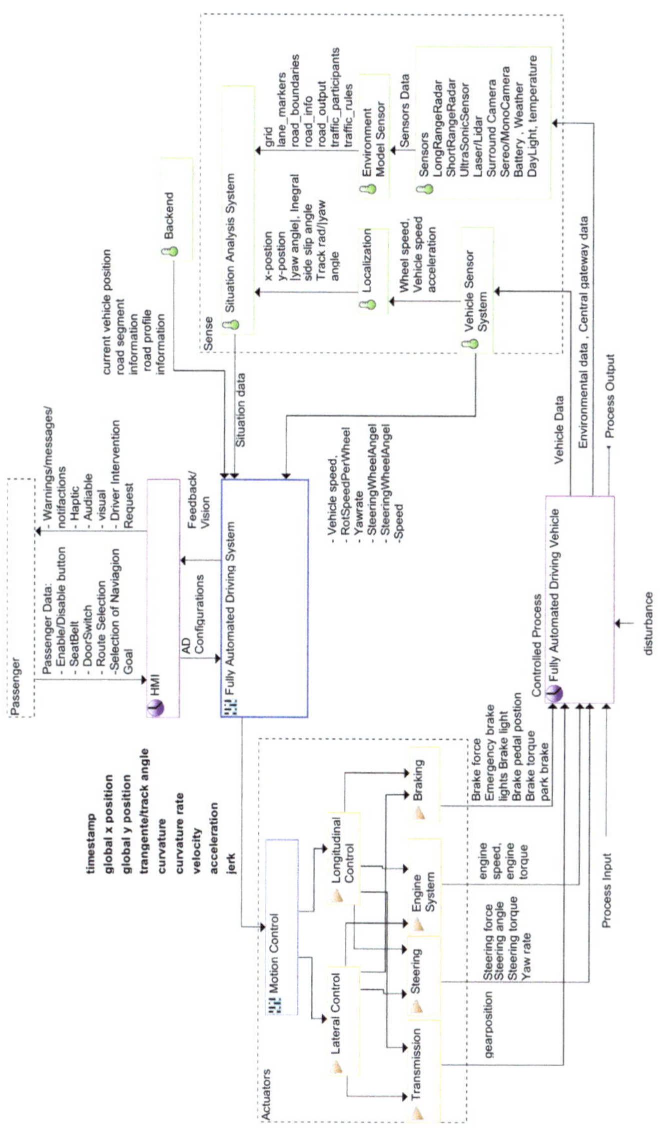

Figure 7.15.: The control structure diagram of the fully automated driving system

Table 7.23.: Examples of potentially unsafe control actions of the automated driving function

Not providing causes hazard	Providing causes hazard	Wrong timing/order causes hazard	Stopped too soon/ applied too long
UCA1.1. The AD system does not provide jerk information while the AD vehicle is approaching in the lane and there is a vehicle in the front. **[H-31, [H-54]**	**UCA1.2.** The AD function provides incorrect data of jerk (rate of change of acceleration) while the AD vehicle in a critical situation. **[H-31,H-46, H-55]**	The AD function provides the jerk data too late while the AD vehicle is approaching in a critical situation **Not Hazardous**	N/A
UCA1.3. The AD system does not provide the velocity at the given trajectory point while AD vehicle is moving too fast. **[H-32, H-33, H-49]**	The AD function provides incorrect velocity at the given trajectory point when the AD vehicle is moving too fast. **[Not Hazardous]**	**UCA1.4.** The AD function provides the velocity too late while the AD vehicle is moving in the lane **[H-54, H-56]**	N/A

We evaluated each of these control actions to check whether or not they lead to hazardous events. We identified 29 unsafe control actions. For example, the unsafe control action *UCA-1: The fully automated driving system does not provide a valid trajectory to motion control while the automated driving vehicle is approaching too fast in the lane, **Hazard Category: control hazards***. This unsafe control action can lead to the control hazard category (e.g. loss of steering or braking or acceleration). Table 7.23 shows examples of the potentially unsafe control actions of the automated driving system.

Table 7.24.: Examples of corresponding software safety constraints at system level

UCA ID	ID	Corresponding Safety Constraints
UCA1.1	SR1.1	The AD vehicle must always provide jerk to motion control while the vehicle is moving.
UCA1.2	SR1.2	The AD vehicle must not provide the value of jerk out of the range data.
UCA1.3	SR1.3	The AD vehicle must provide always the velocity of the vehicle at the given trajectory.
UCA1.4	SR1.4	The AD vehicle shall provide the value of velocity on time to the motion control while AD vehicle is moving.

We translated each hazardous control actions into a corresponding safety requirement such as *SR-1: The automated driving system must always provide a trajectory to motion control.*

To refined the unsafe control actions, we identified the process model variables of the fully automated driving system (shown in Figure. 7.16) at this level. The fully automated driving function has 9 process model variables such as:

- **Road type** with values: road change, parking, intersection, city, mountain, highway, urban or work area.
- **Detection objects** with values: none, obstacle, pedestrian, person, animal, lane, vehicle, motorcycle, bicycle, or road construction.
- **current velocity** with values: $== 0$, > 0, < 240, or unknown.
- **Road map**: received, not received or unknown.
- **Backend status** with values: connected or disconnected, or unknown.
- **Location data** with values: received, not received, or unknown.
- **Environment** with values: flat-road, bi-directions road, hill road, curved road , or non-flat road.
- **Vehicle status** with values: stop, move, park, wait or unknown.

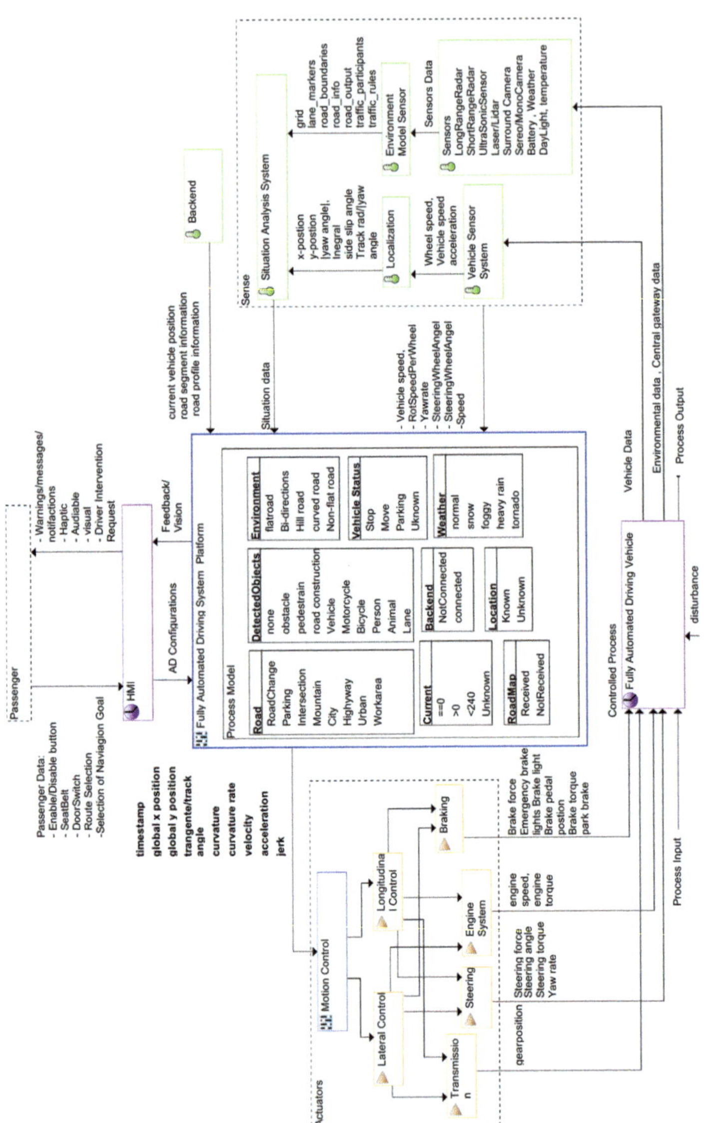

Figure 7.16.: The control structure diagram of the fully automated driving system with process model variables

Table 7.25.: Examples of refined software safety constraints based on process model variables

RUCA	ID	Refined Software Safety Constraints	LTL
RUCA1.1	RSSR1.1	The acceleration command must not be provided anytime when environment is Bi-directions road and current velocity is greater than 0 and RoadMap is NotReceived and DetectedObject is obstacle and weather is snow and Location is unknown and Backend is connected and road is RoadChang and Vehicle Status is Move	LTL1.1
RUCA1.2	RSSR1.2	acceleration command must not be provided too early when environment is Bi-directions road and current Velocity is greater than 0 and RoadMap is NotReceived and DetectedObjects is obstacle and weather is snow and Location is unkonwn and backend is connected and Road is RoadChang and Vehicle Status is Move	LTL1.2

- **Weather** with values: normal, snow, fogy, heavy raining, tornado or unknown.

We used XSTAMPP to generate the context tables, provide a minimal set of combinations between the process model variables and refine unsafe control actions. As a result, we identified 129 refined unsafe control actions which are translated automatically into 129 software safety requirements. For example, a refined unsafe control action *RUCA-1.1 is: the AD system provided an acceleration command while the vehicle is moving on highway and there is a traffic and the roadmap data from the backend is unknown (missing)*. We used the result of this step to refine the software safety requirements. Table 7.25 shows examples of refined software safety requirements based on process model variables. We used the result of this step to refine the software safety requirements.

We determined the causal scenarios (potential causes) for each unsafe control action and its refined unsafe control actions to understand how each hazardous

Table 7.26.: Examples of the causal scenarios of the unsafe control action UCA1.1

Unsafe Control Action (UCA1.1): The AD system does not provide jerk information while the AD vehicle is approaching in the lane and there is a vehicle in the front.

Refined Unsafe Control Action (RUCA) 1.1: The AD system does not provide jerk information when the AD vehicle is approaching on highway, weather is snow, there is a vehicle in the front, and the backend is connected.

ID	Causal Scenarios	Safety Constraints
SC.1	The AD system does not receive an accurate data for acceleration rate from the acceleration sensor while the vehicle is moving on highway	The AD system shall receive the acceleration rate data from the acceleration sensor to calculate an accurate value for the jerk information
SC.2	The AD system issues wrong jerk information vehicle to motion controller at the given trajectory point while the vehicle is moving on city.	The AD system shall receive appropriate information which are required to calculate the accurate jerk information to avoid the abrupt/suddenly acceleration of the AD vehicle.

event could occur in the fully automated driving vehicle. For example, a causal scenario of the unsafe control action UCA1.1 is *CS.1: the AD system does not receive the road map data from the backend while the vehicle is moving on highway*. Table 7.26 shows the examples of the causal scenarios for the unsafe control action UCA1.1 *The AD system does not provide jerk information while the AD vehicle is approaching in the lane and there is a vehicle in the front.*

7.3.3.2. Formalising Software Safety Requirements

We used XSTAMPP to automatically transform the refined software safety requirements into formal specification in linear temporal logic to be used in the verification activities. As a result, we transformed the 129 refined software safety requirements into 129 LTL formulae.. Table 7.27 shows examples of the LTL formulae of the refined software safety constraints.

Table 7.27.: Examples of the corresponding LTL specifications of the software safety requirements

ID	LTL Formulas
RSSR1.1	G (((((Environment==Bi-directions road) &&(CurrentVelocity > 0) &&(RoadMap== NotReceived)&&(DetectedObject==none) && (Weather==snow) &&(Location==Unknown) && (Backend==connected) &&(Road==RoadChange) && (VehicleStatus==Move)))→ (!((controlAction==acceleration)))))
RSSR1.2	G ((((controlAction== acceleration)) → (((!((controlAction ==acceleration)))U(((Environment== Bi-directions road)&&(Current Velocity>0) && (RoadMap==NotReceived) && (DetectedObjects ==none) &&(Weather==snow)&&(Location==Unknown) &&(Backend==connected) &&(Road==RoadChange)&& (Vehicle Status ==Move))))))

7.3.4. Discussion

In this case study, we explored the application of the STPA SwISs approach in identifying the unsafe scenarios for autonomous vehicles in complex environments and deriving software safety requirements to evaluate the current architectural design of the fully automated driving vehicles at Continental. The results showed that STPA is a powerful hazard analysis technique which provides a systematic guidance on deriving detailed safety requirements and develop safety concepts. We also provided the formal specification of the STPA-generated software safety requirements to be used in the formal verification activities of the prototype of full automated vehicle at the design and implementation stages. The results of this case study are used as an assessment report to developers team of the fully automated vehicle at Continental to help them to evaluate the architectural design of the new fully automated driving vehicle at an early stage of the development process. The *STPA SwISs* is currently being used at Continental to assess the current architecture of the fully automated driving vehicle during the whole development process.

7.4. Summary

We presented the empirical validation of the proposed approach. This chapter presents three case studies which were conducted to illustrate and evaluate the application of the STPA SwISs approach during the development process of a new safe software and on the existing software system in the industry. On case study was as a pilot case study to develop a simulator for an adaptive cruise control system with *Adaptive Cruise Control System with Stop-and-Go* function at our institute of software technology, software engineering group, university of Stuttgart. The second case study was conducted on an existing software system like Active Cruise Control System (ACC) with stop-and-go function at BMW Group. The third case study was conducted to illustrate the application of the proposed approach on more complex software system such as the current project of fully automated driving of the self-driving vehicle at Continental. The results from these case studies showed that the STPA SwISs approach is effective, highly scalable and applicable in terms of identifying software safety requirements, automatically transforming them into formal specification in LTL and automatically verifying the software design and implementation against them.

CHAPTER 8

CONCLUSIONS

8.1. Summary

This dissertation presents a comprehensive safety engineering approach based on STPA called STPA for software-intensive systems (*STPA SwISs*). STPA SwISs combines safety analysis, formal verification and *Safety-based Testing* activities to develop safe software. STPA SwISs intends to demonstrate the application of STPA to the software components in a system to derive detailed software safety requirements, transform them into a formal specification in LTL and generate safety-based test cases directly from the results of STPA safety analysis. The STPA SwISs approach allows the software and safety engineers to work together during the software development for safety-critical systems. Moreover, it highlights the advantages of applying STPA to software at the system level to identify potentially unsafe control actions of software and to derive the corresponding safety requirements that prevent software to transition into a hazardous state. The proposed approach is general and can be applied to any software; however, because the software development process as described in the safety standard *ISO 26262 (Road vehicles functional safety)* [ISOv] is subdivided into sub-phases according to the V-Model, we believe that our approach can especially be adapted to be used in the context of this standard as a means to support the development of safe automotive software or to evaluate existing automotive safety-critical software.

We also provided some degree of automation to the *STPA SwISs* approach activities. We also showed how to automatically transform the informal textual safety requirements into formal specification in LTL to enable the verification activities of the system against the STPA-generated safety requirements. We also discussed how to model the STPA results (e.g. process model and the STPA-generated safety requirements) in a suitable model to enable the generation safety-based test cases directly from the STPA safety analysis. We developed an extensible STAMP platform called XSTAMPP as tool support designed specifically to serve the widespread adoption and use of STPA in different areas. We implemented and provided the automation algorithms in the XSTAMPP safety engineering tool to reduce the effort required to generate manually the context tables, refine the unsafe control actions, generate unsafe software scenarios and the software safety requirements and perform verification activities. To simplify the verification and testing activities and reduce the required efforts, we linked between the XSTAMPP safety engineering tool and the model checkers such as NuSMV and SPIN. Furthermore, we developed a safety-based testing tool as an Eclipse plug-in to automatically generate safety-based test cases directly from the STPA results. The safety-based testing tool is integrated within XSTAMPP.

We also demonstrated the application of the proposed approach and the tool support within three case studies: a pilot case study and two industrial case studies based on the automotive software systems.

8.2. Lessons learned

In the following, we presented the lessons learned from the STPA SwISs and the case studies which are presented in this dissertation:

- The work here shows that the STPA approach is very effective on real software systems and applicable to the software component level by deriving detailed software safety requirements at the system level.
- The STPA SwISs approach provides a concept on how to place STPA into the software development process to identify the software safety requirements at the system level and verify software against the STPA-generated software safety requirements at the design level and the implementation phases to help the software and safety engineers to early recognize the software risks.
- The manual writing of the formal specification of the informal textual safety requirements for complex software systems can be impractical for large systems and increases the time and effort required to write them. For this issue, STPA SwISs shows how to automatically transform the informal

software safety requirements into formal specification in LTL to directly enable the verification activities with model checkers.

- Modeling the information derived during the safety analysis into the software behavioral model is a big challenge, due to the different specifications and notations of the safety analysis and the software behavior models. Furthermore, they are usually documented and visualized by different tools. The STPA SwISs approach tackles this issue and provides an algorithm which explains in detail how to model the STPA results into the software behavioral model and how to check the validation and correctness of the software behavioral model against the information derived during the safety analysis process.
- Typically, test engineers build a test model from the software specification and use this model to generate test cases. However, the proof and check of the correctness of this model remains a big challenge and time consuming. Therefore, STPA SwISs provides an algorithm on how to check the correctness of the safe test model which is constructed from the safety analysis results by the safe test engineers. The idea here is to automatically transform the safe test model into an SMV model. Then, the safety engineers will use the SMV model as an input to the model checker to verify its correctness and check whether it satisfies the STPA safety analysis specification which are expressed into formal specification in LTL.
- The complexity of systems makes the software verification activities difficult in practice. The formal verification approaches (e.g. model checker) used in software design and development phase to mechanically prove that the software meets its formal requirements. The formal verification approaches can only prove the presence of the errors and not their absence. However, not all the software errors can cause safety-critical issues. For this issue, we developed and implemented an algorithm to enable the verification activities of the software safety requirements derived during safety analysis with the model checkers.

- The software model checkers do not easily scale up to larger-size software programs and they are limited in the types of errors they can find [Lev09]. In addition, the software testing is very expensive task in the software development process, typically it takes more than 50% of the development time and requires large effort [UL07]. Furthermore, it is difficult to test software completely. Thus, the STPA SwISs approach uses the concept of combining the model checking and testing approaches for testing purpose to verify the software against its software safety requirements instead testing all software behaviors. The idea behind that is to generate safety-based test cases for each STPA-generated software safety requirement to focus the testing effort in a special way to test only the highly dangerous software scenarios which are derived during the STPA safety analysis. This, in turn, shall reduce the required time of testing and help the software and safety engineers to reduce the associated software risks to a lower level.
- The safety-based test cases which are automatically generated from the STPA safety analysis results help us to test the software system against each software safety requirement at the system level. We also believe that the safety-based test cases can help software and safety engineers to test their software components at the system level and recognize the dangerous behavior early in the development process of the safety-critical systems.

8.3. Limitations

In the following, we presented the limitations of the STPA SwISs approach:

- The STPA Step 2 (causal factor analysis) aims to identify accident scenarios that explain how unsafe control actions might occur and how safe control actions might not be followed or executed. Moreover, this step helps in identifying non-trivial safety requirements which are not addressed in the STPA Step 1 (identify Unsafe Control Actions) by analysing the control loop parts. In this step, the safety analyst uses the classification of control flaws leading to hazards (e.g. unsafe control algorithms or unsafe input higher, incorrect process model implementation, etc.) to identify the accident causes for each unsafe control action and develop a detailed informal safety requirements. This step stills need a formal procedure on how to document the accident scenarios based on the results of the STPA step 1 (e.g. unsafe control actions) and the process model variables to easily transform them into formal specification. Therefore, our approach does not transform the results of STPA Step 2 into formal specifications. There are still manual interventions required in this step to be performed by safety and software engineers to manually transform the STPA Step 2 results into formal specification in LTL/CTL.

- Constructing a safe behavioral model from the STPA safety results by safety test engineers depends on the level of information which is handled during the STPA safety analysis process (e.g. process model, and process model variables and values) by safety analyst and how this information describes the software states, interaction and environmental variables which have an effect on the safety of providing the control action by a software controller in the control structure diagram. Furthermore, visualizing the safe behavioral model in Simulink editor requires user expertise in the modeling dynamic behavior to map the safety analysis specification into the Simulink Stateflow specification. Therefore, this point remains as a future work to automatically provide a basic structure of the safe behavioral model from the process model information (e.g. states and its hierarchical levels) which is visualized in XSTAMPP. This will help the safety tester to understand the relationship between the critical system states, environmental and interaction variables which are documented in the process model of the software controller in the control structure diagram.
- Applying STPA SwISs to an existing software system requires that the safety analyst has to first look to the software controller specification (e.g. safety-critical control actions, critical states, and safety-critical variables) to use them to document the process model variables of the software controller in the control structure diagram to reduce the time and effort to correct and verify the safe behavioral model with model checkers.

8.4. Future Work

There are still many interesting directions and trends to extend this work which are described as follows:

8.4.1. Using STPA and STPA SwISs in Compliance with ISO 26262

The main scope of ISO 26262 is to avoid E/E failures. It provides a safety life cycle and stipulates a new functional safety procedure for each new system. ISO 26262 is well regarded by industry and is seen as necessary. The current ISO 26262 document does not mandate the use of specific techniques or methods for safety analysis during the concept phase. It also neither mandates any hazard analysis technique nor gives concrete guidance on how to identify and classify hazards in systems. Reliability analysis approaches such as Fault Tree Analysis (FTA), Failure Mode and Effects Analysis (FMEA) and Hazard and Operability Analysis (HAZOP) are being used for this purpose in the most recent ISO 26262 applications to identify and eliminate hazards. However, these techniques have limitations in identifying hazards in complex systems. Accordingly, there is a need for investigating the effectiveness of other hazard analysis techniques which include more types of hazardous causes such as STPA (System-Theoretic Process Analysis) that can provide more effective guidance on how to identify and eliminate hazards in the design for developing safe systems. We believe that STPA can be used as a hazard analysis in the ISO 26262-part 3, concept phase to identify hazards in the design and develop the functional safety concept.

Furthermore, STPA SwISs is an STPA-based approach for software safety. It is general, which can be applied to any software; however, because the software development process as described in the safety standard ISO 26262 is subdivided into sub-phases according to the V-Model, we believe that our approach can especially be adapted to be used in the context of this standard as a mean to support the development of safe automotive software or to evaluate existing automotive safety-critical software.

8.4.2. Visualization of the STPA Results

STPA uses a control structure diagram to visualize the main components of the system (e.g., controllers, actuators, controlled Processes, and Sensors). Each controller in the control structure diagram must contain a model of the assumed state of the controlled process, called the process model [Lev11]. STPA SwISs shows how to automatically generate the unsafe scenarios based on the process model variables. Furthermore, the STPA SwISs approach introduces a model called safe behavioral model which is directly constructed from the STPA results. This model is used to automatically generate the safety-based test cases. Thus, we found a research potential resulting from our work to visualize the STPA-generated unsafe scenarios and execute them on this model to help the safety analyst to understand how the system will violate the safety constraints.

8.4.3. Using STPA SwISs Results for Auto Safe Code Generation

STPA SwISs shows how to generate the safe behavioral model from the STPA results (e.g. control structure diagram, process model and safety constraints). This model is transformed to the verification model to enable the verification activities and generate safety-based test cases for each STPA-generated safety constraints. The model is visualized in the Simulink Stateflow editor which provides a feature to automatically generate the corresponding code in the C programming language. However, this editor is a commercial tool. Therefore, there is a potential to develop a systematic approach and an open source tool based on the concept of STPA SwISs and its tool support to automate generating safe code directly from the results of the STPA safety analysis. That will help the safety and software engineers to provide a prototype of their thoughts at an earlier stage of the development process of a safe software.

8.4.4. New Improvements to the Tool Support

As a future work, we plan to improve the tool support by considering the other Stateflow semantics which were not addressed in our approach such as the inner transitions and connection and the history junction transitions. Furthermore, we plan to improve the process model in the control structure diagram by allowing the safety analyst to define the data type of each process model variable and draw the multi-hierarchy levels of the process model variables. In the automotive domain, the system architecture is normally created in an architecture tool (e.g. Rhapsody[1], Enterprise Architect[2], and PREEvision[3]). The creation of the functional safety concept includes the mapping of the functional safety requirements to an architectural element. To assign the functional safety requirements to an architectural element, the requirements are exchanged by the standard exchange interface "RIF" between DOORS [4] and PREEvision. Within the PREEvision the requirements are then allocated to the architectural elements. Therefore, we plan to link between XSTAMPP with the architectural tool such as PREEVision to link the results of STPA safety analysis directly to the architectural element.

.

[1]http://www-03.ibm.com/software/products/en/ratirhapfami
[2]http://www.sparxsystems.com/products/ea/
[3]http://vector.com/vi_preevision_en.html
[4]http://www-03.ibm.com/software/products/en/ratidoor

Bibliography

[Abd+16] A. Abdulkhaleq, S. Wagner, D. Lammering, J. Röder, N. Balbierer, L. Ramsauer, T. Raste, and H. Boehmert. "A Systematic Approach Based on STPA for Developing a Dependable Architecture for Fully Automated Driving Vehicles." In: *Procedia Engineering* (2016) (cit. on pp. 164, 167).

[ABM98] P. E. Ammann, P. E. Black, and W. Majurski. "Using Model Checking to Generate Tests from Specifications." In: *Proceedings of the Second IEEE International Conference on Formal Engineering Methods*. ICFEM '98. Washington, DC, USA: IEEE Computer Society, 1998, pp. 46– (cit. on p. 46).

[AD97] L. Apfelbaum and J. Doyle. "Model Based Testing." In: *Software Quality Week Conference*. 1997, pp. 296–300 (cit. on pp. 49, 50).

[AK86] K. R. Apt and D. C. Kozen. "Limits for automatic verification of finite-state concurrent systems." In: *Information Processing Letters* 22.6 (1986), pp. 307–309 (cit. on p. 49).

[Alb+99] D. Alberico, J. Bozarth, M. Brown, J. Gill, S. Mattern, and A. McKinlay VI. *Software System Safety Handbook: A Technical and Managerial Team Approach*. Joint Services Software Safety Committee. 1999 (cit. on p. 25).

[AW14a] A. Abdulkhaleq and S. Wagner. "A-STPA: Open Tool Support for System-Theoretic Process Analysis." In: *2014 STAMP Conference at MIT* (2014) (cit. on p. 113).

[AW14b] A. Abdulkhaleq and S. Wagner. "A Software Safety Verification Method Based on System-Theoretic Process Analysis." In: *Computer Safety, Reliability, and Security: SAFECOMP 2014 Workshop: SASSUR. Florence, Italy, September 8-9, 2014. Proceedings*. Cham: Springer International Publishing, 2014, pp. 401–412 (cit. on pp. 27, 67).

[AW15a] A. Abdulkhaleq and S. Wagner. "Integrated Safety Analysis Using Systems-Theoretic Process Analysis and Software Model Checking." In: *Computer Safety, Reliability, and Security: 34th International Conference, SAFECOMP 2015, Delft, The Netherlands, September 23-25, 2015, Proceedings*. Cham: Springer International Publishing, 2015, pp. 121–134 (cit. on pp. 27, 67, 73, 115).

[AW15b] A. Abdulkhaleq and S. Wagner. "XSTAMPP: An eXtensible STAMP platform as tool support for safety engineering." In: 2015 STAMP Conference, MIT, 2015 (cit. on pp. 109, 142).

[AW16] A. Abdulkhaleq and S. Wagner. "XSTAMPP 2.0: New Improvements to XSTAMPP including CAST Accident Analysis and Extended Approach to STPA." In: 2016 STAMP Conference, MIT, 2016 (cit. on pp. 115, 118, 123).

[AWL15] A. Abdulkhaleq, S. Wagner, and N. Leveson. "A Comprehensive Safety Engineering Approach for Software-Intensive Systems Based on STPA." In: *Proceedings of the 3rd European STAMP Workshop*. Vol. 128. Procedia Engineering, 2015, pp. 2 –11 (cit. on pp. 5, 27, 57, 67).

[Bac90] R. J. R. Back. "Refinement calculus, part II: Parallel and reactive programs." In: Berlin, Heidelberg: Springer Berlin Heidelberg, 1990, pp. 67–93 (cit. on p. 58).

[BCS02] P. Bieber, C. Castel, and C. Seguin. "Combination of fault tree analysis and model checking for safety assessment of complex system." In: *European Dependable Computing Conference*. Springer. 2002, pp. 19–31 (cit. on p. 58).

[Bei95] B. Beizer. *Black-box Testing: Techniques for Functional Testing of Software and Systems*. New York, NY, USA: John Wiley & Sons, Inc., 1995 (cit. on p. 49).

[BK08] C. Baier and J.-P. Katoen. *Principles of Model Checking (Representation and Mind Series)*. The MIT Press, 2008 (cit. on p. 45).

[BKB99] C. Banphawatthanarak, B. H. Krogh, and K. Butts. "Symbolic verification of executable control specifications." In: *Computer Aided Control System Design, 1999. Proceedings of the 1999 IEEE International Symposium on*. IEEE. 1999, pp. 581–586 (cit. on p. 60).

[BKL08] C. Baier, J. Katoen, and K. Larsen. *Principles of Model Checking*. MIT Press, 2008 (cit. on p. 45).

[Bou+97] C. Bourhfir, R. Dssouli, E. Aboulhamid, and N. Rico. "Automatic executable test case generation for extended finite state machine protocols." In: *Testing of Communicating Systems: IFIP TC6 10th International Workshop on Testing of Communicating Systems, 8–10 September 1997, Cheju Island, Korea*. Ed. by M. Kim, S. Kang, and K. Hong. Boston, MA: Springer US, 1997, pp. 75–90 (cit. on p. 63).

[Bro+05] M. Broy, B. Jonsson, J.-P. Katoen, M. Leucker, and A. Pretschner. *Model-Based Testing of Reactive Systems: Advanced Lectures (Lecture Notes in Computer Science)*. Secaucus, NJ, USA: Springer-Verlag New York, Inc., 2005 (cit. on p. 53).

[BV06] M. Bozzano and A. Villafiorita. "The FSAP/NuSMV-SA Safety Analysis Platform." In: *International Journal on Software Tools for Technology Transfer* 9.1 (2006), pp. 5–24 (cit. on p. 59).

[Cav+10] R. Cavada, A. Cimatti, A. C. Jochim, G. Keighren, E. Olivetti, M. Pistore, M. Roveri, and A. Tchaltsev. *NuSMV 2.6 User Manual*. 2010 (cit. on pp. 47, 93, 94).

[CD06] C. Chen and J. S. Dong. "Applying Timed Interval Calculus to Simulink Diagrams." In: *Formal Methods and Software Engineering, 8th International Conference on Formal Engineering Methods, ICFEM 2006, Macao, China, November 1-3, 2006, Proceedings*. 2006, pp. 74–93 (cit. on p. 60).

[CE82] E. M. Clarke and E. A. Emerson. "Design and Synthesis of Synchronization Skeletons Using Branching-Time Temporal Logic." In: *Logic of Programs, Workshop*. London, UK, UK: Springer-Verlag, 1982, pp. 52–71 (cit. on p. 45).

[CG12] A. Calvagna and A. Gargantini. "T-wise Combinatorial Interaction Test Suites Construction Based on Coverage Inheritance." In: *Softw. Test. Verif. Reliab.* 22.7 (Nov. 2012), pp. 507–526 (cit. on p. 54).

[Che+12] C. Chen, J. Sun, Y. Liu, J. S. Dong, and M. Zheng. "Formal modeling and validation of Stateflow diagrams." In: *STTT* 14.6 (2012), pp. 653–671 (cit. on p. 61).

[Cim+00] A. Cimatti, E. Clarke, F. Giunchiglia, and M. Roveri. "NUSMV: a new symbolic model checker." English. In: *International Journal on Software Tools for Technology Transfer* 2.4 (2000), pp. 410–425 (cit. on pp. 28, 47, 58–61, 143).

[Cim+10] A. Cimatti, M. Roveri, A. Susi, and S. Tonetta. "Formalization and validation of safety-critical requirements." In: *arXiv preprint arXiv:1003.1741* (2010) (cit. on p. 48).

[CK93] K.-T. Cheng and A. S. Krishnakumar. "Automatic Functional Test Generation Using The Extended Finite State Machine Model." In: *Design Automation, 1993. 30th Conference on*. 1993, pp. 86–91 (cit. on p. 51).

[CR02] R. Castanet and D. Rouillard. "Generate Certified Test Cases by Combining Theorem Proving and Reachability Analysis." In: Boston, MA: Testing of Communicating Systems XIV: Application to Internet Technologies and Services, Springer US, 2002, pp. 249–265 (cit. on p. 53).

[Dal+99] S. R. Dalal, A. Jain, N. Karunanithi, J. M. Leaton, C. M. Lott, G. C. Patton, and B. M. Horowitz. "Model-based Testing in Practice." In: *Proceedings of the 21st International Conference on Software Engineering*. Los Angeles, California, USA: ACM, 1999, pp. 285–294 (cit. on p. 49).

[Erd+14] G. Erdogan, Y. Li, R. K. Runde, F. Seehusen, and K. Stølen. "Approaches for the combined use of risk analysis and testing: a systematic literature review." In: *International Journal on Software Tools for Technology Transfer* 16.5 (2014), pp. 627–642 (cit. on p. 55).

[Eri05] C. A. Ericson. *Hazard analysis techniques for system safety*. Wiley Hoboken, NJ, 2005, 499 p. (Cit. on pp. 33, 41, 42).

[Fer+12] O. Ferrante, L. Benvenuti, L. Mangeruca, C. Sofronis, and A. Ferrari. "Parallel NuSMV: A NuSMV Extension for the Verification of Complex Embedded Systems." In: *Computer Safety, Reliability, and Security: SAFECOMP 2012 Workshops: Sassur, ASCoMS, DESEC4LCCI, ERCIM/EWICS, IWDE, Magdeburg, Germany, September 25-28, 2012. Proceedings*. Berlin, Heidelberg: Springer Berlin Heidelberg, 2012, pp. 409–416 (cit. on p. 61).

[Fer88] T. S. Ferry. *Modern Accident Investigation and Analysis*. Wiley, 1988 (cit. on p. 32).

[Fid+98] C. J. Fidge, I. J. Hayes, A. P. Martin, and A. Wabenhorst. "A Set-Theoretic Model for Real-Time Specification and Reasoning." In: *Proceedings of the Mathematics of Program Construction*. MPC '98. London, UK, UK: Springer-Verlag, 1998, pp. 188–206 (cit. on p. 60).

[FLR78] A. Frimtzis, M. Lipow, and D. Reifer. "Software Failure Modes and Effects Analysis." In: *Industry/SAMSO Conf. and Workshop on Mission Assurance* (1978), pp. 154–154 (cit. on p. 41).

[FM91] K. Forsberg and H. Mooz. "The relationship of system engineering to the project cycle." In: *INCOSE International Symposium*. Vol. 1. 1. Wiley Online Library. 1991, pp. 57–65 (cit. on p. 27).

[FO76] L. D. Fosdick and L. J. Osterweil. "Data Flow Analysis in Software Reliability." In: *ACM Comput. Surv.* 8.3 (Sept. 1976), pp. 305–330 (cit. on p. 63).

[FS14] M. Felderer and I. Schieferdecker. "A taxonomy of risk-based testing." In: *International Journal on Software Tools for Technology Transfer* 16.5 (2014), pp. 559–568 (cit. on p. 55).

[Gil62] A. Gill. *Introduction to the theory of finite-state machines*. McGraw-Hill electronic sciences series. McGraw-Hill, 1962 (cit. on p. 50).

[Har10] T. Hardy. *The System Safety Skeptic: Lessons Learned in Safety Management and Engineering*. AuthorHouse, 2010 (cit. on pp. 31, 42).

[Har12] T. Hardy. *Software and System Safety*. AuthorHouse, 2012 (cit. on p. 42).

[Har87] D. Harel. "Statecharts: a visual formalism for complex systems." In: *Science of Computer Programming* 8.3 (1987), pp. 231 –274 (cit. on pp. 50–52).

[HC12] M. Hinchey and L. Coyle. *Conquering Complexity*. SpringerLink : Bücher. Springer London, 2012 (cit. on p. 49).

[Hei31] H. W. Heinrich. *Industrial Accident Prevention: A Scientific Approach*. New York:McGraw-Hill, 1931 (cit. on p. 32).

[HJS08] Y. Hamadi, S. Jabbour, and L. Sais. "ManySAT: a parallel SAT solver." In: *Journal on Satisfiability, Boolean Modeling and Computation* 6 (2008), pp. 245–262 (cit. on p. 61).

[HN96] D. Harel and A. Naamad. "The STATEMATE Semantics of Statecharts." In: *ACM Trans. Softw. Eng. Methodol.* 5.4 (Oct. 1996), pp. 293–333 (cit. on p. 63).

[Hol03] G. Holzmann. *Spin Model Checker, the: Primer and Reference Manual*. First. Addison-Wesley Professional, 2003 (cit. on pp. 46, 48).

[Hol04] E. Hollnagel. *Barriers and Accident Prevention*. Ashgate, 2004 (cit. on p. 32).

[Hon+00] H. S. Hong, Y. G. Kim, S. D. Cha, D. H. Bae, and H. Ural. "A test sequence selection method for statecharts." In: *Software Testing, Verification and Reliability* 10.4 (2000), pp. 203–227 (cit. on p. 63).

[HR07] G. Hamon and J. Rushby. "An operational semantics for Stateflow." In: *International Journal on Software Tools for Technology Transfer* 9.5-6 (2007), pp. 447–456 (cit. on p. 52).

[HS99] G. J. Holzmann and M. H. Smith. *Software Model Checking – Extracting Verification Models from source code*. 1999 (cit. on pp. 48, 78).

[Isk62] A. P. Iskrant. "The Epidemiologic Approach to Accident Causation." In: *American Journal of Public Health and the Nations Health* 52.10 (1962), pp. 1708–1711 (cit. on p. 32).

[ISOv] ISO. "International Organization for Standardization, International Standard 26262: Road vehicles – Functional safety. International Standard." In: *ISO, First Edition* (Nov. 2011) (cit. on pp. 23, 164, 179).

[Jaf+91] M. S. Jaffe, N. G. Leveson, M. P. E. Heimdahl, and B. E. Melhart. "Software requirements analysis for real-time process-control systems." In: *IEEE Transactions on Software Engineering* 17.3 (1991), pp. 241–258 (cit. on p. 31).

[KHE11] J. Kloos, T. Hussain, and R. Eschbach. "Risk-Based Testing of Safety-Critical Embedded Systems Driven by Fault Tree Analysis." In: *Software Testing, Verification and Validation Workshops (ICSTW), 2011 IEEE Fourth International Conference on*. 2011, pp. 26–33 (cit. on p. 62).

[Kim+99] Y. G. Kim, H. S. Hong, D. H. Bae, and S. D. Cha. "Test cases generation from UML state diagrams." In: *IEE Proceedings - Software* 146.4 (1999), pp. 187–192 (cit. on p. 63).

[KKL13] D. Kuhn, R. Kacker, and Y. Lei. *Introduction to Combinatorial Testing*. Chapman & Hall/CRC Innovations in Software Engineering and Software Development Series. Taylor & Francis, 2013 (cit. on pp. 54, 57, 82, 84, 115–117, 154).

[KLK08] R. Kuhn, Y. Lei, and R. Kacker. "Practical Combinatorial Testing: Beyond Pairwise." In: *IT Professional* 10.3 (2008), pp. 19–23 (cit. on p. 54).

[Kua62] M. K. Kuan. "Graphic programming using odd or even points." In: (1962) (cit. on p. 53).

[LCS91] N. G. Leveson, S. S. Cha, and T. J. Shimeall. "Safety verification of Ada programs using software fault trees." In: *IEEE Software* 8.4 (1991), pp. 48–59 (cit. on p. 48).

[Lev00] N. Leveson. "Completeness in Formal Specification Language Design for Process-control Systems." In: *Proceedings of the Third Workshop on Formal Methods in Software Practice*. FMSP '00. Portland, Oregon, USA: ACM, 2000, pp. 75–87 (cit. on p. 50).

[Lev04a] N. Leveson. "A New Accident Model for Engineering Safer Systems." In: *Safety Science* (2004), pp. 237–270 (cit. on pp. 35, 36).

[Lev04b] N. G. Leveson. "Role of Software in Spacecraft Accidents." In: *Journal of Spacecraft and Rockets* 41.4 (2004), pp. 564–575 (cit. on p. 42).

[Lev09] N. G. Leveson. "Software Challenges in Achieving Space Safety." In: *Journal of the British Interplanetary Society* 62 (2009), pp. 265–272 (cit. on pp. 42, 182).

[Lev11] N. Leveson. *Engineering a Safer World: Systems Thinking Applied to Safety*. Engineering systems. MIT Press, 2011 (cit. on pp. 5, 23, 26, 31, 36–38, 40, 42, 56, 59, 71, 123, 185).

[Lev82] N. G. Leveson. "Software Safety." In: *SIGSOFT Softw. Eng. Notes* 7.2 (Apr. 1982), pp. 21–24 (cit. on p. 33).

[Lev91] N. G. Leveson. "Software Safety in Embedded Computer Systems." In: *Commun. ACM* 34.2 (Feb. 1991), pp. 34–46 (cit. on p. 31).

[Lev95] N. G. Leveson. *Safeware: System Safety and Computers*. New York, NY, USA: ACM, 1995 (cit. on p. 42).

[LH83a] N. G. Leveson and P. R. Harvey. "Analyzing Software Safety." In: *IEEE Transactions on Software Engineering* SE-9.5 (1983), pp. 569–579 (cit. on p. 41).

[LH83b] N. G. Leveson and P. R. Harvey. "Software fault tree analysis." In: *Journal of Systems and Software* 3.2 (1983), pp. 173 –181 (cit. on p. 33).

[LK12] M. Li and R. Kumar. "Model-based automatic test generation for Simulink/Stateflow using extended finite automaton." In: *2012 IEEE International Conference on Automation Science and Engineering (CASE)*. 2012, pp. 857–862 (cit. on p. 65).

[LN05] R. Lutz and A. Nikora. "Failure Assessment." In: *1st International Forum on Integrated System Health Engineering and Management in Aerospace* (2005) (cit. on pp. 33, 34).

[Lut00] R. R. Lutz. “Software Engineering for Safety: A Roadmap.” In: *Proceedings of the Conference on The Future of Software Engineering*. ICSE ’00. Limerick, Ireland: ACM, 2000, pp. 213–226 (cit. on p. 55).

[Mat16] MathWorks. *The MathWorks, Inc. Simulink, 2015. Version R2015b*. 2016 (cit. on pp. 74, 75, 92, 94).

[MBR06] B Meenakshi, A. Bhatnagar, and S. Roy. “Tool for translating simulink models into input language of a model checker.” In: *International Conference on Formal Engineering Methods*. Springer. 2006, pp. 606–620 (cit. on p. 60).

[McD+95] J. A. McDermid, M. Nicholson, D. J. Pumfrey, and P. Fenelon. “Experience with the application of HAZOP to computer-based systems.” In: *Computer Assurance, 1995. COMPASS ’95. Systems Integrity, Software Safety and Process Security. Proceedings of the Tenth Annual Conference on*. 1995, pp. 37–48 (cit. on p. 34).

[McM93] K. L. McMillan. *Symbolic Model Checking*. Norwell, MA, USA: Kluwer Academic Publishers, 1993 (cit. on pp. 27, 46, 47, 60, 143, 145).

[Mea55] G. H. Mealy. “A method for synthesizing sequential circuits.” In: *The Bell System Technical Journal* 34.5 (1955), pp. 1045–1079 (cit. on p. 50).

[NAS10] NASA/SP-2010-580. *NASA System Safety Handbook, Volume 1, System Safety Framework and Concepts for Implementation*. NASA, 2010 (cit. on p. 32).

[OLA03] A. J. Offutt, S. Liu, and A. Abdurazik. “Generating Test Data From State-based Specifications.” In: (2003) (cit. on p. 53).

[Ort+04] F. Ortmeier, A. Thums, G. Schellhorn, and W. Reif. “Combining Formal Methods and Safety Analysis – The ForMoSA Approach.” In: *Springer Berlin Heidelberg* 3147 (2004), pp. 474–493 (cit. on p. 59).

[Pas+09] C. S. Pasareanu, J. Schumann, P. Mehlitz, M. Lowry, G. Karsai, H. Nine, and S. Neema. “Model Based Analysis and Test Generation for Flight Software.” In: *Space Mission Challenges for Information Technology, 2009. SMC-IT 2009. Third IEEE International Conference on*. 2009, pp. 83–90 (cit. on p. 64).

[Pnu77] A. Pnueli. “The Temporal Logic of Programs.” In: *Proceedings of the 18th Annual Symposium on Foundations of Computer Science*. SFCS ’77. Washington, DC, USA: IEEE Computer Society, 1977, pp. 46–57 (cit. on pp. 27, 45, 46, 67).

[Pre00] R. S. Pressman. *Software Engineering (3rd Ed.): A Practitioner’s Approach*. New York, NY, USA: McGraw-Hill, Inc., 2000 (cit. on p. 49).

[Pre01] A. Pretschner. “Classical Search Strategies for Test Case Generation with Constraint Logic Programming.” In: *In Proc. Formal Approaches to Testing of Software*. BRICS, 2001, pp. 47–60 (cit. on p. 53).

[Pro03] S. J. Prowell. "JUMBL: a tool for model-based statistical testing." In: *System Sciences, 2003. Proceedings of the 36th Annual Hawaii International Conference on*. 2003, 9 pp.– (cit. on p. 53).

[Qur08] Z. H. Qureshi. *A Review of Accident Modelling Approaches for Complex Critical Sociotechnical Systems*. Tech. rep. Australian Government Department of Defence - Defence Science and Technology Organisation, 2008 (cit. on p. 32).

[Rau13] M. Rausand. *Risk Assessment: Theory, Methods, and Applications*. Statistics in Practice. Wiley, 2013 (cit. on p. 33).

[Rea90] J. Reason. "The Contribution of Latent Human Failures to the Breakdown of Complex Systems." In: *Philosophical Transactions of the Royal Society of London. B, Biological Sciences* 1241 (Apr. 1990), pp. 475–484 (cit. on p. 33).

[Rea97] J. Reason. *Managing the risks of organizational accidents*. English. Ashgate Aldershot, 1997, xvii, 252 p. : (cit. on p. 33).

[Red04] F. Redmill. "Exploring Risk-based Testing and Its Implications: Research Articles." In: *Softw. Test. Verif. Reliab.* 14.1 (Mar. 2004), pp. 3–15 (cit. on p. 62).

[Rei79] D. J. Reifer. "Software Failure Modes and Effects Analysis." In: *IEEE Transactions on Reliability* R-28.3 (1979), pp. 247–249 (cit. on p. 41).

[RH08] P. Runeson and M. Höst. "Guidelines for conducting and reporting case study research in software engineering." In: *Empirical Software Engineering* 14.2 (2008), pp. 131–164 (cit. on p. 143).

[RHP06] J. Reason, E. Hollnagel, and J. Paries. "Revisiting the Swiss Cheese Model of Accidents." In: *Journal of Clinical Engineering* 27 (2006), pp. 110–115 (cit. on p. 33).

[Rit10] N. Ritter. "Understanding a widely misunderstood statistic: Cronbach's alpha." In: *in Southwestern Educational Research Association (SERA)* (2010).

[Roz11] K. Y. Rozier. "Linear temporal logic symbolic model checking." In: *Computer Science Review* 5.2 (2011), pp. 163–203 (cit. on p. 46).

[SAE03] SAE. *Adaptive Cruise Control Operating Characteristics and User Interface*. SAE Standard J2399. 2003 (cit. on pp. 23, 125).

[SK09] B. Schlich and S. Kowalewski. "Model checking C source code for embedded systems." In: *International Journal on Software Tools for Technology Transfer* 11.3 (2009), pp. 187–202 (cit. on p. 48).

[SP15] S. Sharvia and Y. Papadopoulos. "Integrating model checking with HiP-HOPS in model-based safety analysis." In: *Reliability Engineering and System Safety* 135 (2015), pp. 64 –80 (cit. on p. 59).

[ST99] K. Sere and E. Troubitsyna. "Safety Analysis in Formal Specification." In: *Proceedings of the Wold Congress on Formal Methods in the Development of Computing Systems-Volume II*. FM '99. London, UK, UK: Springer-Verlag, 1999, pp. 1564–1583 (cit. on p. 58).

[Sun+09a] J. Sun, Y. Liu, J. S. Dong, and C. Chen. "Integrating specification and programs for system modeling and verification." In: *Theoretical Aspects of Software Engineering, 2009. TASE 2009. Third IEEE International Symposium on*. IEEE, 2009, pp. 127–135 (cit. on p. 61).

[Sun+09b] J. Sun, Y. Liu, J. S. Dong, and J. Pang. "PAT: Towards flexible verification under fairness." In: *International Conference on Computer Aided Verification*. Springer. 2009, pp. 709–714 (cit. on p. 61).

[Tho13] J. Thomas. "Extending and automating a systems-theoretic hazard analysis for requirements generation and analysis." PhD thesis. MIT, Apr. 2013 (cit. on pp. 23, 39–41, 57, 69).

[TL11] J. Thomas and G. N. Leveson. "Performing Hazard Analysis on Complex, Software- and Human-Intensive Systems." In: *In 29th International System Safety Conference* (2011) (cit. on p. 39).

[TLM02] A. C. Tribble, D. L. Lempia, and S. P. Miller. "Software safety analysis of a flight guidance system." In: *Digital Avionics Systems Conference, 2002. Proceedings. The 21st*. Vol. 2. 2002, 13C1–1–13C1–10 vol.2 (cit. on p. 58).

[Tra+99] N. Tracey, J. Clark, J. McDermid, and K. Mander. "Integrating safety analysis with automatic test-data generation for software safety verification." In: *Proceedings of the 17th International Conference on System Safety*. 1999, pp. 128–137 (cit. on p. 48).

[UL07] M. Utting and B. Legeard. *Practical Model-Based Testing: A Tools Approach*. San Francisco, CA, USA: Morgan Kaufmann Publishers Inc., 2007 (cit. on pp. 51, 182).

[UML04] UML. *Unified Modeling Language Specification*. Version 2.0. Object Management Group (OMG). 2004 (cit. on p. 50).

[Ura87] H. Ural. "Test sequence selection based on static data flow analysis." In: *Computer Communications* 10.5 (1987), pp. 234 –242 (cit. on p. 63).

[Ves+81] W. Vesely, F. F Goldberg, N. H. Roberts, and D. Hassl. *Fault Tree Handbook Nureg-0492*. U.S. Nuclear Regulatory Commission, 1981 (cit. on pp. 5, 25, 33, 55).

[VN00] P. Venhovens and A. B. Naab K. "Stop and go cruise control." In: *Seoul 2000 FISITA World Automotive Congress* 2000 (2000), p. 396 (cit. on pp. 23, 126).

[Win09] A. Windisch. "Search-based testing of complex simulink models containing stateflow diagrams." In: *Software Engineering - Companion Volume, 2009. ICSE-Companion 2009. 31st International Conference on*. 2009, pp. 395–398 (cit. on p. 64).

[Wir+08] M. Wirsing, J.-P. Banâtre, M. Hölzl, and A. Rauschmayer, eds. *Software-Intensive Systems and New Computing Paradigms: Challenges and Visions*. Berlin, Heidelberg: Springer-Verlag, 2008 (cit. on p. 25).

[Won+10] W. E. Wong, V. Debroy, A. Surampudi, H. Kim, and M. F. Siok. "Recent Catastrophic Accidents: Investigating How Software was Responsible." In: *Secure Software Integration and Reliability Improvement (SSIRI), 2010 Fourth International Conference on*. 2010, pp. 14–22 (cit. on p. 5).

[ZC08] Y. Zhan and J. A. Clark. "A Search-based Framework for Automatic Testing of MATLAB/Simulink Models." In: *J. Syst. Softw.* 81.2 (Feb. 2008), pp. 262–285 (cit. on p. 64).

[Zim+09] F. Zimmermann, R. Eschbach, J. Kloss, and T. Bauer. "Risk-based Statistical Testing: A refinement-based approach to the reliability analysis of safety-critical systems." In: *Proceedings of the Spring TAV Workshop* (2009) (cit. on p. 62).

[FME67] FMECA. "Design Analysis Procedure For Failure Modes, Effects and Criticality Analysis (FMECA)." In: *Society for Automotive Engineers* (1967) (cit. on pp. 25, 34, 55).

[JPL00] JPL. *Report of the Loss of the Mars Polar Lander and Deep Space 2 Missions*. 2000 (cit. on p. 25).

[Mil49] Military, U.S. *MIL-P-1629 Procedures for Performing a Failure Modes Effects and Criticality Analysis*. 1949 (cit. on pp. 5, 34).

[Min91] Minister of Defence. *Hazard Analysis and Safety Classificaiton of the Computer and Programmable Electronic System Elements of Defence Equipment, Interim Defence Standard 00-56, Issue 1*. 1991 (cit. on p. 25).

[NAS04] NASA-GB- 8719.13. *NASA Software Safety Guidebook*. NASA, 2004 (cit. on pp. 23, 55).

[Tro68] Troyan, J.E and Le Vine, L.Y. "HAZOP, Loss Prevention, 2: 125." In: (1968) (cit. on pp. 25, 34).

All URLs were last checked on 15.12.2016.

ACC SIMULATOR

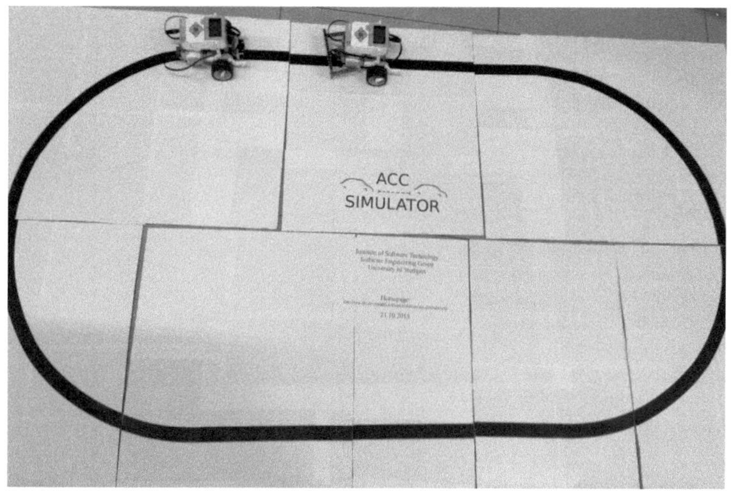

Figure A.1.: The Simulator of ACC system with Stop-and-Go function

A.1. The C Code of the ACC Simulator

```
//*****************************************
//ACCwithstopandGoSimulator.c
//-------------------
//We created this program in C and tested with Lego mindstrom EV3
//*****************************************
//-------------------
#include <stdio.h>
#include <stdlib.h>
#include <unistd.h>
```

```
#include <string.h>
#include <math.h>
#include <time.h>
#include <stdbool.h>

#define accoff (1)
#define standby (2)
#define resume (3)
#define cruise (4)
#define follow (5)
#define stop (6)
#define accelerate (1)
#define decelerate (2)
#define fullystop (3)
#define keepspeed (4)
#define unknown (5)
//*****************************************
// GLOBAL VARIABLES

double d_frontspeed = 15.458; //20.3194;
double d_currentspeed = 0;
double d_safedistance = 20;
double d_frontdistance = -1;
int frontspeed = 15; //20.3194;
int currentspeed = 0;
int safedistance = 20;
int frontdistance = -1;
int states = accoff;
int controlAction=unknown;
int decelerationratio = 2;
int accelerationratio = 4;
double d_initialspeed = 1;
double d_desiredspeed = 20.416; //25.1805; // Deg/s (40% of max speed)
double d_deltaX;
double d_minimumSpeed = 1.22;
double d_timeGap = 0.3;
double d_temp;
double d_safetyTimeGap = 0.9;
int initialspeed = 1;
int desiredspeed = 20; //25.1805; // Deg/s (40% of max speed)
int deltaX;
int minimumSpeed = 1;
int timeGap = 0;
int temp;
int safetyTimeGap = 1;
\\*****************************
```

```

 void calcTimeGap() {
if (d_currentspeed > 0) {
d_timeGap = (d_frontdistance/d_currentspeed);
} else {
d_timeGap = 0;
}
timeGap = (int)floor(d_timeGap);
}

void accelerate_f() {
if (states != cruise && states != resume){
d_currentspeed += calPID(sqrt( fabs(
(d_currentspeed * d_currentspeed) + 2 * fabs((d_deltaX + d_safetyTimeGap) − d_timeGap
        )))−d_currentspeed);
} else {
d_currentspeed = d_currentspeed;
}
if (states == resume) {
d_currentspeed += accelerationratio;
}

if (d_currentspeed > d_desiredspeed) {
d_currentspeed = d_desiredspeed;
}
currentspeed = (int)d_currentspeed;
}
 void decelerate_f() {
d_currentspeed −= calPID(sqrt( fabs(
(d_currentspeed * d_currentspeed) + 2.7 * fabs(d_deltaX + d_safetyTimeGap − d_timeGap
        )))−d_currentspeed);
if (d_currentspeed <= 0) {
d_currentspeed = 0;
} else if (d_currentspeed > d_desiredspeed) {
d_currentspeed = d_desiredspeed;
}
currentspeed = (int)floor(d_currentspeed);
}
void goMove(){
if (states != follow) {
accelerate_f();
if (states == stop) {
d_currentspeed = 0;
currentspeed = (int)floor(d_currentspeed);
}
} else if (states == follow) {
```

```
decelerate_f();
}
 (int)((d_currentspeed/17.593)*360);
}
 int GetSonarRawValue()
{
 r = (rand() % 250);
return r;
}

int main()
{
states = standby;
controlAction=unknown;
d_currentspeed = d_initialspeed;
currentspeed = (int)floor(d_currentspeed);
int i = 1;
while(i < 300)
{
d_frontdistance = GetSonarRawValue();
frontdistance = (int)floor(d_frontdistance);
 if (d_frontdistance <= −1) {
d_frontdistance = 250;
frontdistance = (int)floor(d_frontdistance);
}
 calcTimeGap();
d_deltaX = 0.5+sqrt(d_timeGap);
deltaX = (int)floor(d_deltaX);
if (deltaX < 0) {
d_deltaX = 0;
deltaX = 0;
} else if (deltaX > 10) {
d_deltaX = 10;
deltaX = 10;
} }
 if (states == standby) {
if (d_currentspeed > d_minimumSpeed) {
states = resume;
controlAction=accelerate;
}
} else if (states == resume) {
if (d_timeGap < (d_deltaX + d_safetyTimeGap) && d_timeGap != 0) {
states = follow;
controlAction=decelerate;
} else if (d_currentspeed == d_desiredspeed && d_timeGap > d_safetyTimeGap) {
states = cruise;
```

```
controlAction=keepspeed;
} else if (d_timeGap == 0) {
states = stop;
controlAction=fullystop;
} else if (d_currentspeed < d_desiredspeed && d_timeGap > d_safetyTimeGap) {
states = resume;
controlAction=accelerate;
}
} else if (states == cruise) {
if (d_timeGap > (d_deltaX + d_safetyTimeGap) && d_currentspeed == d_desiredspeed) {
states = cruise;
controlAction=keepspeed;
} else if (d_timeGap < (d_deltaX + d_safetyTimeGap)) {
states = follow;
controlAction=decelerate;
} else if (d_currentspeed < d_desiredspeed && d_timeGap > (d_deltaX + d_safetyTimeGap
    )) {
states = resume;
controlAction=accelerate;
 }
} else if (states == follow) {
if (d_timeGap > (d_deltaX + d_safetyTimeGap) && d_frontdistance > 10) {
states = resume;
controlAction=accelerate;
} else if (d_timeGap <= d_safetyTimeGap && d_frontdistance < 10) {
states = stop;
controlAction=fullystop;
}
} else if (states == stop) {
if (d_timeGap > d_safetyTimeGap || d_frontdistance > 10) {
states = resume;
controlAction=accelerate;    }
}
goMove();
return 0;
}
```

A.2. The SMV Model of ACC Simulator

```
--############################################
--This model is automtically generated by STPA TCGenerator tool which is developed by Asim Abdulkhaleq, Stefan Wagner
--University of Stuttgart, Institute of Software Technology, Germany
--Copyright (c) 2016, at Institute of Software Technology, Software Engineering Group -2016
--Date/Time:2016/02/16 17:57:08

--############################################


MODULE Sub_ControlSpeed(Power,currentspeed,desriedspeedIn,timeGap,deltaX,minimumSpeed,safetyTimeGap,frontdistance,controlAction,initialspeed,accelerationratio,frontdistance_in,Ignited,desiredspeed)
VAR

states: {resume ,cruise ,follow ,stop };
ASSIGN

init (states):=resume;

next (states):=case
TRUE:{resume};
states=resume & (currentspeed < desiredspeed & timeGap > safetyTimeGap) : resume;
states=cruise & (timeGap > (deltaX + safetyTimeGap) & currentspeed = desiredspeed) : cruise;
states=cruise & (currentspeed < desiredspeed & timeGap > (deltaX + safetyTimeGap)) : resume;
states=resume & (currentspeed = desiredspeed & timeGap > safetyTimeGap) : cruise;
states=follow & (timeGap > (deltaX + safetyTimeGap) & frontdistance > 10) : resume;
states=cruise & (timeGap < (deltaX + safetyTimeGap)) : follow;
states=stop & (timeGap > safetyTimeGap | frontdistance > 10) : resume;
states=resume & (timeGap = 0) : stop;
states=resume & (timeGap < (deltaX + safetyTimeGap) & timeGap != 0) : follow;
states=follow & ((timeGap <= safetyTimeGap & frontdistance < 10 )) : stop;
TRUE: {resume ,cruise ,follow ,stop };
esac;

MODULE Sub_ACCActive(Power,currentspeed,desriedspeedIn,timeGap,deltaX,minimumSpeed,safetyTimeGap,frontdistance,controlAction,initialspeed,accelerationratio,frontdistance_in,Ignited,desiredspeed)
VAR

```

```
ControlSpeed:Sub_ControlSpeed(Power,currentspeed,desriedspeedIn,timeGap,deltaX,
        minimumSpeed,safetyTimeGap,frontdistance,controlAction,initialspeed,
        accelerationratio,frontdistance_in,Ignited,desiredspeed);

states: {ControlSpeed ,ReadSensorData };
ASSIGN
init (states):=ReadSensorData;
MODULE Sub_ACCOn(Power,currentspeed,desriedspeedIn,timeGap,deltaX,minimumSpeed
        ,safetyTimeGap,frontdistance,controlAction,initialspeed,accelerationratio,
        frontdistance_in,Ignited,desiredspeed)
VAR
ACCActive:Sub_ACCActive(Power,currentspeed,desriedspeedIn,timeGap,deltaX,
        minimumSpeed,safetyTimeGap,frontdistance,controlAction,initialspeed,
        accelerationratio,frontdistance_in,Ignited,desiredspeed);
states: {ACCActive ,standby };
ASSIGN
init (states):=ACCActive;
next (states):=case
TRUE:{standby};
states=standby & (currentspeed<minimumSpeed) : standby;
states=standby & (currentspeed>minimumSpeed) : ACCActive;
states=ACCActive & (currentspeed< minimumSpeed) : standby;
TRUE: {ACCActive ,standby };
esac;

MODULE main
VAR
Power: boolean;
currentspeed: 0..10 ;
desriedspeedIn: 0..10 ;
timeGap: 0..10 ;
deltaX: 0..10 ;
minimumSpeed: 0..10 ;
safetyTimeGap: 0..10 ;
frontdistance: 0..10 ;
controlAction:{fullystop,accelerate,decelerate};
initialspeed: 0..10 ;
accelerationratio: 0..10 ;
frontdistance_in: 0..10 ;
Ignited: boolean;
desiredspeed: 0..10 ;

ACCOn:Sub_ACCOn(Power,currentspeed,desriedspeedIn,timeGap,deltaX,minimumSpeed,
        safetyTimeGap,frontdistance,controlAction,initialspeed,accelerationratio,
        frontdistance_in,Ignited,desiredspeed);
```

```
states: {ACCOff ,ACCOn };
ASSIGN
init (states):=ACCOff;
init (Power) := FALSE ;
init (currentspeed) := 0 ;
init (desriedspeedIn) := 0 ;
init (timeGap) := 0 ;
init (deltaX) := 0 ;
init (minimumSpeed) := 0 ;
init (safetyTimeGap) := 0 ;
init (frontdistance) := 0 ;
init (initialspeed) := 0 ;
init (accelerationratio) := 0 ;
init (frontdistance_in) := 0 ;
init (Ignited) := FALSE ;
init (desiredspeed) := 0 ;

next (Ignited ):=case
states =ACCOff :Power;
states =ACCOff :Power;
TRUE:Ignited;
esac;
next (accelerationratio ):=case
states =standby : 4;
states =standby : 4;
TRUE:accelerationratio;
esac;
next (minimumSpeed ):=case
states =standby :2;
states =standby :2;
TRUE:minimumSpeed;
esac;
next (desiredspeed ):=case
states =standby :desriedspeedIn;
states =standby :desriedspeedIn;
TRUE:desiredspeed;
esac;
next (safetyTimeGap ):=case
states =standby :2;
states =standby :2;
TRUE:safetyTimeGap;
esac;
next (currentspeed ):=case
states =standby : initialspeed;
states =resume : currentspeed + 4;
states =cruise : desiredspeed;
```

```
states =follow : currentspeed −1;
states =stop :0;
states =resume : currentspeed + 4;
states =cruise : desiredspeed;
states =follow : currentspeed −1;
states =stop :0;
states =standby : initialspeed;
TRUE:currentspeed;
esac;
next (frontdistance ):=case
states =ReadSensorData : frontdistance_in ;
states =ReadSensorData : frontdistance_in ;
TRUE:frontdistance;
esac;
next (controlAction ):=case
states =resume :accelerate;
states =follow :decelerate;
states =stop :fullystop;
states =resume :accelerate;
states =follow :decelerate;
states =stop :fullystop;
TRUE:controlAction;
esac;
next (timeGap ):=case
states =resume & frontdistance > 0 : currentspeed/frontdistance;
states =resume & frontdistance > 0 : currentspeed/frontdistance;
TRUE:timeGap;
esac;
next (deltaX ):=case
states =resume & 4 > 0 : 1+ timeGap/4;
states =resume & 4 > 0 : 1+ timeGap/4;
TRUE:deltaX;
esac;
next (states):=case
TRUE:{ACCOff};
states=ACCOff & (Ignited) : ACCOn;
states=ACCOn & (!Ignited) : ACCOff;
TRUE: {ACCOff ,ACCOn };
esac;
```

A.3. The Promela Model of ACC Source Code

```
// Generated by MODEX Version 2.8 – 20 February 2015 by Asim Abdulkhaleq
// Sat Apr 16 15:02:24 2016 from ACCSimulator.c

#define accoff (1)
#define standby (2)
#define resume (3)
#define cruise (4)
#define follow (5)
#define stop (6)
#define accelerate (1)
#define decelerate (2)
#define fullystop (3)
#define keepspeed (4)
#define unknown (5)

c_state "long res_p_main" "Global"
bool lck_p_main_ret;
bool lck_p_main;
c_state "long res_p_GetSonarRawValue" "Global"
bool lck_p_GetSonarRawValue_ret;
bool lck_p_GetSonarRawValue;
c_state "long res_p_goMove" "Global"
bool lck_p_goMove_ret;
bool lck_p_goMove;
c_state "long res_p_decelerate_f" "Global"
bool lck_p_decelerate_f_ret;
bool lck_p_decelerate_f;
c_state "long res_p_accelerate_f" "Global"
bool lck_p_accelerate_f_ret;
bool lck_p_accelerate_f;
c_state "long res_p_calcTimeGap" "Global"
bool lck_p_calcTimeGap_ret;
bool lck_p_calcTimeGap;
c_state "double par0_calPID" "Global"
c_state "long res_p_calPID" "Global"
bool lck_p_calPID_ret;
bool lck_p_calPID;
int r;
c_state "double kd " "Global" "0.1"
c_state "double ki " "Global" "0.1"
c_state "double kp " "Global" "0.1"
c_state "double output" "Global"
c_state "double preverror " "Global" "0"
```

```
c_state "double error" "Global"
c_state "double minvalue " "Global" "0"
c_state "double maxvalue " "Global" "200"
c_state "double deltatime " "Global" "0.01"
c_state "double derivativegain" "Global"
c_state "double integralgain " "Global" "0"
c_state "double epsilon " "Global" "0.01"
int safetyTimeGap = 1;
int temp;
int timeGap = 0;
int minimumSpeed = 1;
int deltaX;
int desiredspeed = 20;
int initialspeed = 1;
c_state "double d_safetyTimeGap " "Global" "0.9"
c_state "double d_temp" "Global"
c_state "double d_timeGap " "Global" "0.3"
c_state "double d_minimumSpeed " "Global" "1.22"
c_state "double d_deltaX" "Global"
c_state "double d_desiredspeed " "Global" "20.416"
c_state "double d_initialspeed " "Global" "1"
int accelerationratio = 4;
int decelerationratio = 2;
int controlAction = 5;
int states = 1;
int frontdistance = (−1);
int safedistance = 20;
int currentspeed = 0;
int frontspeed = 15;
c_state "double d_frontdistance " "Global" "(−1)"
c_state "double d_safedistance " "Global" "20"
c_state "double d_currentspeed " "Global" "0"
c_state "double d_frontspeed " "Global" "15.458"
chan ret_p_main = [1] of { pid };
chan exc_cll_p_main = [0] of { pid };
chan req_cll_p_main = [1] of { pid };
chan ret_p_GetSonarRawValue = [1] of { pid };
chan exc_cll_p_GetSonarRawValue = [0] of { pid };
chan req_cll_p_GetSonarRawValue = [1] of { pid };
chan ret_p_goMove = [1] of { pid };
chan exc_cll_p_goMove = [0] of { pid };
chan req_cll_p_goMove = [1] of { pid };
chan ret_p_decelerate_f = [1] of { pid };
chan exc_cll_p_decelerate_f = [0] of { pid };
chan req_cll_p_decelerate_f = [1] of { pid };
chan ret_p_accelerate_f = [1] of { pid };
```

```
chan exc_cll_p_accelerate_f = [0] of { pid };
chan req_cll_p_accelerate_f = [1] of { pid };
chan ret_p_calcTimeGap = [1] of { pid };
chan exc_cll_p_calcTimeGap = [0] of { pid };
chan req_cll_p_calcTimeGap = [1] of { pid };
chan ret_p_calPID = [1] of { pid };
chan exc_cll_p_calPID = [0] of { pid };
chan req_cll_p_calPID = [1] of { pid };
c_state "double diff" "Local p_calPID"
active proctype p_calPID( )
{
pid lck_id;
endRestart:
atomic {
nempty(req_cll_p_calPID) && !lck_p_calPID -> lck_p_calPID = 1;
req_cll_p_calPID?lck_id; exc_cll_p_calPID?eval(lck_id);
c_code { Pp_calPID->diff = now.par0_calPID; };
lck_p_calPID = 0;
};
c_code { now.error=Pp_calPID->diff; };
if
:: c_expr { (now.error>now.epsilon) };
c_code { now.integralgain+=(now.error*now.deltatime); };
:: c_expr { !(now.error>now.epsilon) };
fi;
c_code { now.derivativegain+=((now.error-now.preverror)/now.deltatime); };
c_code { now.output=(((now.kp*now.error)+(now.ki*now.integralgain))+(now.kd*now.
        derivativegain)); };
if
:: c_expr { (now.output>now.maxvalue) };
c_code { now.output=now.maxvalue; };
:: c_expr { !(now.output>now.maxvalue) };
if
:: c_expr { (now.output<now.minvalue) };
c_code { now.output=now.minvalue; };
:: c_expr { !(now.output<now.minvalue) };
fi;
fi;
c_code { now.preverror=now.error; };
c_code { now.d_temp=now.output; };
c_code { now.temp=(int )floor(now.d_temp); };
atomic { !lck_p_calPID_ret -> lck_p_calPID_ret = 1 };
c_code { now.res_p_calPID = (long) now.output; }; goto Return;
Return: skip;
ret_p_calPID!lck_id;
goto endRestart
```

```
}
active proctype p_calcTimeGap()
{
pid lck_id;
endRestart:
atomic {
nempty(req_cll_p_calcTimeGap) && !lck_p_calcTimeGap -> lck_p_calcTimeGap = 1;
req_cll_p_calcTimeGap?lck_id; exc_cll_p_calcTimeGap?eval(lck_id);
lck_p_calcTimeGap = 0;
};
if
:: c_expr { (now.d_currentspeed>0) };
c_code { now.d_timeGap=(now.d_frontdistance/now.d_currentspeed); };
:: c_expr { !(now.d_currentspeed>0) };
c_code { now.d_timeGap=0; };
fi;
c_code { now.timeGap=(int )floor(now.d_timeGap); };
Return: skip;
ret_p_calcTimeGap!lck_id;
goto endRestart
}
active proctype p_accelerate_f()
{
pid lck_id;
endRestart:
atomic {
nempty(req_cll_p_accelerate_f) && !lck_p_accelerate_f -> lck_p_accelerate_f = 1;
req_cll_p_accelerate_f?lck_id; exc_cll_p_accelerate_f?eval(lck_id);
lck_p_accelerate_f = 0;
};
if
:: c_expr { ((now.states!=4)&&(now.states!=3)) };
atomic {
lck_p_calPID == 0 && empty(req_cll_p_calPID) -> req_cll_p_calPID!_pid;
c_code { now.par0_calPID = (sqrt(fabs(((now.d_currentspeed*now.d_currentspeed)+(2*
        fabs(((now.d_deltaX+now.d_safetyTimeGap)-now.d_timeGap))))))-now.
        d_currentspeed); };
exc_cll_p_calPID!_pid;
}
ret_p_calPID?eval(_pid);
c_code { now.d_currentspeed+= now.res_p_calPID; now.lck_p_calPID_ret = 0; };
:: c_expr { !((now.states!=4)&&(now.states!=3)) };
c_code { now.d_currentspeed=now.d_currentspeed; };
fi;
if
:: c_expr { (now.states==3) };
```

```
c_code { now.d_currentspeed+=now.accelerationratio; };
:: c_expr { !(now.states==3) };
fi;
if
:: c_expr { (now.d_currentspeed>now.d_desiredspeed) };
c_code { now.d_currentspeed=now.d_desiredspeed; };
:: c_expr { !(now.d_currentspeed>now.d_desiredspeed) };
fi;
c_code { now.currentspeed=(int )now.d_currentspeed; };
Return: skip;
ret_p_accelerate_f!lck_id;
goto endRestart
}
active proctype p_decelerate_f()
{
pid lck_id;
endRestart:
atomic {
nempty(req_cll_p_decelerate_f) && !lck_p_decelerate_f -> lck_p_decelerate_f = 1;
req_cll_p_decelerate_f?lck_id; exc_cll_p_decelerate_f?eval(lck_id);
lck_p_decelerate_f = 0;
};
atomic {
lck_p_calPID == 0 && empty(req_cll_p_calPID) -> req_cll_p_calPID!_pid;
c_code { now.par0_calPID = (sqrt(fabs(((now.d_currentspeed*now.d_currentspeed)
        +(2.7*fabs(((now.d_deltaX+now.d_safetyTimeGap)-now.d_timeGap))))))-now.
        d_currentspeed); };
exc_cll_p_calPID!_pid;
}
ret_p_calPID?eval(_pid);
c_code { now.d_currentspeed-= now.res_p_calPID; now.lck_p_calPID_ret = 0; };
if
:: c_expr { (now.d_currentspeed<=0) };
c_code { now.d_currentspeed=0; };
:: c_expr { !(now.d_currentspeed<=0) };
if
:: c_expr { (now.d_currentspeed>now.d_desiredspeed) };
c_code { now.d_currentspeed=now.d_desiredspeed; };
:: c_expr { !(now.d_currentspeed>now.d_desiredspeed) };
fi;
fi;
c_code { now.currentspeed=(int )floor(now.d_currentspeed); };
Return: skip;
ret_p_decelerate_f!lck_id;
goto endRestart
}
```

```
active proctype p_goMove()
{
pid lck_id;
endRestart:
atomic {
nempty(req_cll_p_goMove) && !lck_p_goMove -> lck_p_goMove = 1;
req_cll_p_goMove?lck_id; exc_cll_p_goMove?eval(lck_id);
lck_p_goMove = 0;
};
if
:: c_expr { (now.states!=5) };
atomic {
lck_p_accelerate_f == 0 && empty(req_cll_p_accelerate_f) -> req_cll_p_accelerate_f!
        _pid;
exc_cll_p_accelerate_f!_pid;
}
ret_p_accelerate_f?eval(_pid);
c_code { ; now.lck_p_accelerate_f_ret = 0; };
if
:: c_expr { (now.states==6) };
c_code { now.d_currentspeed=0; };
c_code { now.currentspeed=(int )floor(now.d_currentspeed); };
:: c_expr { !(now.states==6) };
fi;
:: c_expr { !(now.states!=5) };
if
:: c_expr { (now.states==5) };
atomic {
lck_p_decelerate_f == 0 && empty(req_cll_p_decelerate_f) -> req_cll_p_decelerate_f!
        _pid;
exc_cll_p_decelerate_f!_pid;
}
ret_p_decelerate_f?eval(_pid);
c_code { ; now.lck_p_decelerate_f_ret = 0; };
:: c_expr { !(now.states==5) };
fi;
fi;
Return: skip;
ret_p_goMove!lck_id;
goto endRestart
}
active proctype p_GetSonarRawValue()
{
pid lck_id;
endRestart:
atomic {
```

```
nempty(req_cll_p_GetSonarRawValue) && !lck_p_GetSonarRawValue ->
        lck_p_GetSonarRawValue = 1;
req_cll_p_GetSonarRawValue?lck_id; exc_cll_p_GetSonarRawValue?eval(lck_id);
lck_p_GetSonarRawValue = 0;
};
c_code { now.r=(rand()%250); };
atomic { !lck_p_GetSonarRawValue_ret -> lck_p_GetSonarRawValue_ret = 1 };
c_code { now.res_p_GetSonarRawValue = (long) now.r; }; goto Return;
Return: skip;
ret_p_GetSonarRawValue!lck_id;
goto endRestart
}
active proctype p_main()
{
int i = 1;
pid lck_id;
c_code { now.states=2; };
c_code { now.controlAction=5; };
c_code { now.d_currentspeed=now.d_initialspeed; };
c_code { now.currentspeed=(int )floor(now.d_currentspeed); };
L_0:
do
:: c_expr { (Pp_main->i<300) };
atomic {
lck_p_GetSonarRawValue == 0 && empty(req_cll_p_GetSonarRawValue) ->
        req_cll_p_GetSonarRawValue!_pid;
exc_cll_p_GetSonarRawValue!_pid;
}
ret_p_GetSonarRawValue?eval(_pid);
c_code { now.d_frontdistance= now.res_p_GetSonarRawValue; now.
        lck_p_GetSonarRawValue_ret = 0; };
c_code { now.frontdistance=(int )floor(now.d_frontdistance); };
if
:: c_expr { (now.d_frontdistance<=(-1)) };
c_code { now.d_frontdistance=250; };
c_code { now.frontdistance=(int )floor(now.d_frontdistance); };
:: c_expr { !(now.d_frontdistance<=(-1)) };
fi;
atomic {
lck_p_calcTimeGap == 0 && empty(req_cll_p_calcTimeGap) -> req_cll_p_calcTimeGap!
        _pid;
exc_cll_p_calcTimeGap!_pid;
}
ret_p_calcTimeGap?eval(_pid);
c_code { ; now.lck_p_calcTimeGap_ret = 0; };
c_code { now.d_deltaX=(0.5+sqrt(now.d_timeGap)); };
```

```
c_code { now.deltaX=(int )floor(now.d_deltaX); };
if
:: c_expr { (now.deltaX<0) };
c_code { now.d_deltaX=0; };
c_code { now.deltaX=0; };
:: c_expr { !(now.deltaX<0) };
if
:: c_expr { (now.deltaX>10) };
c_code { now.d_deltaX=10; };
c_code { now.deltaX=10; };
:: c_expr { !(now.deltaX>10) };
fi;
fi;
if
:: c_expr { (now.states==2) };
if
:: c_expr { (now.d_currentspeed>now.d_minimumSpeed) };
c_code { now.states=3; };
c_code { now.controlAction=1; };
:: c_expr { !(now.d_currentspeed>now.d_minimumSpeed) };
fi;
:: c_expr { !(now.states==2) };
if
:: c_expr { (now.states==3) };
if
:: c_expr { ((now.d_timeGap<(now.d_deltaX+now.d_safetyTimeGap))&&(now.
        d_timeGap!=0)) };
c_code { now.states=5; };
c_code { now.controlAction=2; };
:: c_expr { !((now.d_timeGap<(now.d_deltaX+now.d_safetyTimeGap))&&(now.
        d_timeGap!=0)) };
if
:: c_expr { ((now.d_currentspeed==now.d_desiredspeed)&&(now.d_timeGap>now.
        d_safetyTimeGap)) };
c_code { now.states=4; };
c_code { now.controlAction=4; };
:: c_expr { !((now.d_currentspeed==now.d_desiredspeed)&&(now.d_timeGap>now.
        d_safetyTimeGap)) };
if
:: c_expr { (now.d_timeGap==0) };
c_code { now.states=6; };
c_code { now.controlAction=3; };
:: c_expr { !(now.d_timeGap==0) };
if
:: c_expr { ((now.d_currentspeed<now.d_desiredspeed)&&(now.d_timeGap>now.
        d_safetyTimeGap)) };
```

```
c_code { now.states=3; };
c_code { now.controlAction=1; };
:: c_expr { !((now.d_currentspeed<now.d_desiredspeed)&&(now.d_timeGap>now.
      d_safetyTimeGap)) };
fi;
fi;
fi;
fi;
:: c_expr { !(now.states==3) };
if
:: c_expr { (now.states==4) };
if
:: c_expr { ((now.d_timeGap>(now.d_deltaX+now.d_safetyTimeGap))&&(now.
      d_currentspeed==now.d_desiredspeed)) };
c_code { now.states=4; };
c_code { now.controlAction=4; };
:: c_expr { !((now.d_timeGap>(now.d_deltaX+now.d_safetyTimeGap))&&(now.
      d_currentspeed==now.d_desiredspeed)) };
if
:: c_expr { (now.d_timeGap<(now.d_deltaX+now.d_safetyTimeGap)) };
c_code { now.states=5; };
c_code { now.controlAction=2; };
:: c_expr { !(now.d_timeGap<(now.d_deltaX+now.d_safetyTimeGap)) };
if
:: c_expr { ((now.d_currentspeed<now.d_desiredspeed)&&(now.d_timeGap>(now.
      d_deltaX+now.d_safetyTimeGap))) };
c_code { now.states=3; };
c_code { now.controlAction=1; };
:: c_expr { !((now.d_currentspeed<now.d_desiredspeed)&&(now.d_timeGap>(now.
      d_deltaX+now.d_safetyTimeGap))) };
fi;
fi;
fi;
:: c_expr { !(now.states==4) };
if
:: c_expr { (now.states==5) };
if
:: c_expr { ((now.d_timeGap>(now.d_deltaX+now.d_safetyTimeGap))&&(now.
      d_frontdistance>10)) };
c_code { now.states=3; };
c_code { now.controlAction=1; };
:: c_expr { !((now.d_timeGap>(now.d_deltaX+now.d_safetyTimeGap))&&(now.
      d_frontdistance>10)) };
if
:: c_expr { ((now.d_timeGap<=now.d_safetyTimeGap)&&(now.d_frontdistance<10)) };
c_code { now.states=6; };
```

```
c_code { now.controlAction=3; };
:: c_expr { !((now.d_timeGap<=now.d_safetyTimeGap)&&(now.d_frontdistance<10)) };
fi;
fi;
:: c_expr { !(now.states==5) };
if
:: c_expr { (now.states==6) };
if
:: c_expr { ((now.d_timeGap>now.d_safetyTimeGap)||(now.d_frontdistance>10)) };
c_code { now.states=3; };
c_code { now.controlAction=1; };
:: c_expr { !((now.d_timeGap>now.d_safetyTimeGap)||(now.d_frontdistance>10)) };
fi;
:: c_expr { !(now.states==6) };
fi; fi; fi; fi;
fi;
atomic {
lck_p_goMove == 0 && empty(req_cll_p_goMove) -> req_cll_p_goMove!_pid;
exc_cll_p_goMove!_pid;
}
ret_p_goMove?eval(_pid);
c_code { ; now.lck_p_goMove_ret = 0; };
c_code { Printf("%i\n",Pp_main->i); };
c_code { Pp_main->i=(Pp_main->i+1); };
goto L_0;
:: c_expr { !(Pp_main->i<300) }; -> break
od;
atomic { !lck_p_main_ret -> lck_p_main_ret = 1 };
c_code { now.res_p_main = (long) 0; }; goto Return;
Return: skip;
}
```